William Blake

William Blake

Morton D Paley

GREENWICH HOUSE
Distributed by Crown Publishers, Inc.
New York

First published 1978 by Phaidon Press Ltd, Oxford,
England.

This 1983 edition is published by Greenwich House,
a division of Arlington House, Inc, distributed
by Crown Publishers, Inc.

Printed in Hong Kong by South China Printing Co.

ISBN 0-517-416506

h g f e d c b a

Contents

Acknowledgements

THE AUTHOR AND PUBLISHERS are grateful to all museum authorities and private owners who have given permission for works in their possession to be reproduced. We would especially like to thank Sir Geoffrey Keynes for allowing us to photograph works in his collection. Figs. 5 and 10, and plates 4, 5, 7, 10, 12, 13–16, 18, 20, 22–4, 27, 35–7, 66, 68, 90, 92, 94, 97–8, 100 and 104 are reproduced by permission of the Trustees of the British Museum, and plate 42 by permission of the British Library Board (Additional MS. 39764). Plates 46, 49, 65, 78, 84 and 86 are Crown Copyright, Victoria and Albert Museum. Fig. 8 and plates 1, 26, 28, 30, 31, 33, 47, 48, 82, 87, 88, 112 and 113 are reproduced by permission of the Trustees of the Tate Gallery; plates 67, 77 and 79 by courtesy of the Glasgow Museums and Art Galleries, Stirling Maxwell Collection, Pollok House; and plate 74 by permission of the Trustees of the Cecil Higgins Art Gallery, Bedford.

Preface

THE ART OF WILLIAM BLAKE has never attracted as much interest as it does today. Yet, despite the voluminous literature on Blake as both poet and artist, there exists no introduction to his work published in a large format with a sufficient number of plates to indicate the rich variety of Blake's production in different modes and in various media. This book is an attempt to remedy that lack. In writing it, I have been painfully aware of how much I owe to other scholars and critics, and how infrequently I could acknowledge these debts if the book were not to turn into an unreadable mass of footnotes. It is hoped, however, that this essay may serve as an introduction to the literature on Blake as well as to Blake's own works.

I have also incurred a number of personal obligations which it is a pleasure to record here. My deepest gratitude goes to Dr David Bindman and to Mr Martin Butlin, both of whom gave generously and patiently of their time and expertise to provide me with information. Any errors in this book are my own; were it not for such help, there would be many more of them. In selecting the plates, I was aided by suggestions from Professor G. E. Bentley, Jr, Professor Morris Eaves, Professor W. J. T. Mitchell, and Dr Gerda Norvig. In locating the pictures reproduced and compiling measurements of them, I was assisted by Miss Sue Warne. Professor John E. Grant, Dr Suzanne Hoover, and Professor Anne K. Mellor provided useful points

of information; Miss Frances Carey helped me more than I can say in my work in the Department of Prints and Drawings of the British Museum. Professor Robert N. Essick kindly shared with me some of his knowledge of Blake's graphic techniques. And the encouragement of Mr Keith Roberts has made the entire project possible.

The author of a study of Blake is presented with an embarrassment of riches in choosing a text, as there exist several excellent editions, each with particular strengths. The desideratum here was a single text that could be cited throughout for both Blake's poetry and his prose, including the letters; and so *The Complete Writings of William Blake*, ed. Geoffrey Keynes (London, Oxford University Press, 1966) was chosen. A list of other works frequently referred to can be found in the Notes to the Text.

Unless otherwise indicated, references to Blake's works in illuminated printing follow *William Blake's Illuminated Books: A Census*, compiled by Geoffrey Keynes and Edwin Wolf II (New York, The Grolier Club, 1953). Thus, for example, '*America*, Copy O, plate 7' refers to the plate beginning 'In thunders ends the voice. Then Albions Angel wrathful burnt' (John Linnell copy, now in the Fitzwilliam Museum).

This book is dedicated to the memory of Professor Edward C. Mack.

M.D.P.

1. To Try All Experiments

ON 11 DECEMBER 1757, William Blake, the son of a hosier, was baptized in 'Grinling Gibbons's ornate font in Wren's noble Palladian church of St James'.[1] Many charming anecdotes of Blake's childhood are told by Gilchrist and others—of how the boy saw angels on Peckham Rye, how his mother beat him for saying he had seen Ezekiel beneath a tree, and how he began to make copies from prints at a very early age.

Our documented knowledge of Blake's artistic career begins when, at the age of ten, he was sent to Henry Pars's drawing school in the Strand, where he would have learned to draw after the antique by copying casts in the traditional manner. Had he remained at Pars's, he could have gone on to the drawing school of the Society of Arts, or he could have been placed with a 'painter of Eminence', according to Frederick Tatham,[2] 'but from the huge premium required, . . . he therefore himself proposed Engraving as being less expensive & sufficiently eligible for his future avocations'.[3] Accordingly in 1772 Blake was apprenticed to James Basire, official engraver to the Society of Antiquaries. This choice was to be of lifelong importance to him for several reasons. Most obviously, it provided him with a means of livelihood. All his working life he sustained himself as a professional engraver, but although he had periods of great expectation, he never attained great success in his profession. The largest sum he ever received for a single plate was, ironically, for one of his first commissions, *The Fall of Rosamund*, for which Macklin paid him £80 in 1783.[4] More typical prices would be the ten guineas each he received from William Hayley for 'Six little plates' for *The Triumphs of Temper*[5] or the four guineas he unsuccessfully asked of R. H. Cromek in proposing to etch[6] a plate after his own dedication drawing for *The Grave*. (Cromek was willing to pay Lewis Schiavonetti ten guineas for a plate after the same dedication drawing.) And although the position of a highly successful engraver like Basire was that of a prosperous burgher presiding over apprentices, most engravers never attained such status but remained, as Blake did throughout his life, lower middle-class

artisans vulnerable to the fluctuations of the market. The Royal Academy in its Instrument of Foundation (1768) did not admit engravers, limiting membership to 'Painters, Sculptors, or Architects'. The engraver was looked upon as a skilled worker rather than as the practitioner of a liberal art. In 1770, with the institution of the new category of Associate, five engravers were admitted as A. R. A.'s; then in 1812 fourteen engravers appealed directly to the Prince Regent on the matter and were answered by the Council: 'With such an important difference in their intellectual pretensions as Artists, it appear'd to the framers of this Society that to admit Engravers into the first class of their Members, would be incompatible with justice and a due regard to the dignity of the Royal Academy.'[7] In choosing this profession Blake had consigned his workaday self to the position of the Spectre of Urthona in *Jerusalem*, whose task is to 'labour obedient' at the furnaces of the inspired artist Los.

The choice of Basire in particular had some further, more particular implications. Basire was indeed a celebrated engraver, but a celebrated engraver of an earlier generation. As Gilchrist puts it, 'He was an engraver well grounded in drawing, of dry, hard, monotonous, but painstakingly conscientious style; the lingering representative of a school already getting old-fashioned, but not without staunch admirers, for its "firm and correct outline", among antiquaries . . .'[8] The coming mode was that of engravers like Francesco Bartolozzi, who employed stipple, dot, and lozenge to create complex effects of light and shade. Blake himself was not above using such techniques, never being as consistent in practice as he seems to us, retrospectively, in theory; but the basis of his technique had the hard linearism of Basire, which was beginning to look as old-fashioned as the flattened-out portraits of Hogarth and Hudson did in comparison to the rich, fully-textured works of Reynolds and Gainsborough. And so Blake began his career by appearing old-fashioned. The public preference for the Bartolozzi style led him later to some aesthetic reflections that are better considered in

FIG. I CATHERINE BLAKE: *Portrait of the Young William Blake.*
About 1827–31. Pencil. 6⅛ × 4⅛ in. Cambridge, Fitzwilliam
Museum

relation to his writings about art, as there is nothing to
indicate that he was conscious of the symbolic implications of these techniques at the time of his apprenticeship.

Another element of Blake's style and, equally, of his
aesthetics, is the Gothic, and this too he derived from
his apprenticeship to Basire. As is well known, Basire
set him to drawing tombs in Westminster Abbey. 'It
kindled a fervent love of the Gothic . . . which lasted his
life', as Gilchrist says,[9] though once more there is nothing to indicate that in these early years the Gothic took
on the theoretical importance for Blake that it assumed
later. The salient fact is that by drawing and engraving
for Gough's *Sepulchral Monuments*, he learned to sympathize profoundly with medieval sculpture and architecture as opposed to the rococo-gothic of Horace
Walpole. There was no disparity between this interest
and a desire to renew the lost art of the Greeks, as
manifested in Blake's contribution of eight plates to
Cumberland's *Thoughts on Outline* in 1794–5. James
Basire, in fact, was also an engraver of Stuart and
Revett's *Antiquities of Athens*, the first volume of which

had appeared in 1762. Probably through his association
with Basire, Blake obtained in 1792 the commission to
execute four plates for volume III of the *Antiquities*. For
him, as for like-minded contemporaries, there was no
contradiction between the Grecian and the Gothic;
both were manifestations of a pure artistic impulse
thought to have become obscured by later accretions
just as Ossian and the poems of Rowley were considered
to be emanations from a less sullied age. This predilec-
tion for the primitive was characteristic of Blake
throughout his life, although the objects of it did not
remain the same.

Blake's taste in print collecting was already well
advanced during the period of his apprenticeship. He
frequented the auction room of Abraham Langford,
who (according to Benjamin Heath Malkin, Blake's
first biographer) 'called him his little connoisseur. . .
He copied Raphael and Michael Angelo, Martin
Hemskerck and Albert Durer, Julio Romano, and the
rest of the historic class, neglecting to buy any other
prints, however celebrated.'[10] Among the engravers
with whose work he would have become familiar at this
early time were Marcantonio Raimondi (whom he
mentions much later, in the 'Public Address'), Julio
Bonasoni, the subject of a pamphlet by George Cumberland published in 1793, and Giorgio Ghisi, seven of
whose engravings after Michelangelo Blake copied as
wash drawings. At this time, however, the work of these
relatively early Italian engravers influenced his ideas
more than it did his execution. For at least twenty years
his engraving style was neither highly original nor
extraordinarily successful, and it is significant that in
the early years of the nineteenth century he was to
return to a number of his early engravings in order to
rework them in his mature style. A striking example is
the engraving of a figure after Michelangelo's *Crucifixion
of St Peter* via a drawing, now unknown, by Salviati
(Gioseffo Porta). Because the print bears the date 1773,
it was once thought to be an example of Blake's pre-
cocious genius. However, there is, as Keynes points
out,[11] an early state of the plate, engraved, Blake wrote,
'when I was a beginner at Basires'. Probably no earlier
than the time of his exhibition of 1809, and possibly
much later, he reworked this plate, adding for example

the sunburst behind the rock and its reflection in the sea, making the figure genuinely powerful, monumental, and pensive. He also added the title *Joseph of Arimathea among The Rocks of Albion*, and an inscription characteristic of his later thought:

> This is One of the Gothic Artists who Built the Cathedrals in what we call the Dark Ages/Wandering about in sheep skins & goat skins. of whom the World was not worthy/such were the Christians in all Ages.

His apprenticeship with Basire had provided him with the materials, both technical and intellectual, for this masterpiece; but some four decades had to pass before the mature work could be created (*Pl. 94*).

Presumably Blake completed his apprenticeship seven years after he began, that is in the summer of 1779. He was now ready to aim for a higher place in the world of art. On 8 October 1779, he was admitted to the Royal Academy as a full student. It is doubtful, however, that he ever took full advantage of the educational opportunities afforded him, as his own anecdote of an encounter with the venerable Keeper, George Moser, indicates:

> I was once looking over the Prints from Rafael & Michael Angelo in the Library of the Royal Academy. Moser came to me & said: 'You should not Study these old Hard, Stiff & Dry, Unfinish'd Works of Art—Stay a little & I will shew you what you should Study.' He then went & took down Le Brun's & Rubens's Galleries. How I did secretly Rage! I also spoke my Mind ... I said to Moser, 'These things that you call Finish'd are not Even Begun; how can they then be Finish'd? The Man who does not know The Beginning never can know the End of Art.'[12]

All were, of course, ready to admire Raphael and Michelangelo, but it was one thing to praise, another to imitate, as Blake wished to do. For the same reason he entirely rejected the examples of his older contemporaries Reynolds and Gainsborough, aligning himself with sublime painting as represented by James Barry, Henry Fuseli, and John Hamilton Mortimer. The figure of Mortimer, who was sixteen years older than Blake, would have bulked especially large to him in 1779, for in that same year Mortimer was elected an

Academician, three of his paintings on medieval subjects were shown in the Annual Exhibition, and he died. Mortimer was known chiefly for the wildness and energy of his subject-matter; later, reading Reynolds's remark on the artist who 'is at last delivered of his monsters, with difficulty and pain', Blake noted: 'A Stroke at Mortimer!'[13] It has been pointed out that Blake's 1795 colour print *Nebuchadnezzar* (*Pl.* 29) is indebted to Mortimer's drawing of Nebuchadnezzar recovering his reason, etched by Blyth in 1781.[14] Mortimer was also the creator of galleries of Shakespearean and Chaucerian characters, a painter of medieval history, and, as in his *Death on a Pale Horse*, an exemplifier of Burke's sublime of terror.[15] Blake was to follow him in all three categories.

Barry, who was of the same age as Mortimer, practised a somewhat different type of sublime painting. His was the heroic sublime of *Philoctetes* and *Lear*, both subjects later undertaken by Blake. Barry's epic series of pictures illustrative of the progress of civilization, executed for the Society of Arts at the Adelphi from 1777 until 1783, later caused Blake to inveigh:

> Who will Dare to Say that Polite Art is Encouraged or Either Wished or Tolerated in a Nation where The Society for the Encouragement of Art Suffer'd Barry to Give them his Labour for Nothing, A Society Composed of the Flower of the English Nobility & Gentry?—Suffering an Artist to Starve while he Supported Really what They, under Pretence of Encouraging, were Endeavouring to Depress.— Barry told me that while he Did that Work, he lived on Bread & Apples.[16]

Here Barry is not so much an individual artist for Blake but the archetype of the true Artist, labouring without pay like the builder of Lord Weary's castle in the ballad of *Lamkin* (actually, Barry was voted two hundred guineas by the Society after the completion of the series). 'Barry told me' indicates personal acquaintance, and it is difficult to believe that Blake did not attend at least some of the lectures delivered by Barry as Professor of Painting from 1782 to 1799. It is clear enough that Blake absorbed something of Barry's rhetoric of indignation as well as his ideas about society's obligation to the arts. There was political sympathy between the two as well,[17] and Barry's pro-Revolutionary engraving *The Phoenix of Liberty* (1776) may be regarded as a forerunner of Blake's *America* (1793). After Barry was expelled from the Royal Academy in 1799, supposedly for insulting other Academicians in his writings and lectures, Blake concluded, 'The really Industrious, Virtuous & Independent Barry is driven out to make room for a pack of Idle Sycophants.'[18] About 1811 he wrote some verses about art 'to come in Barry, a Poem', but apparently the poem was never written.

Fuseli's barbed entries on Barry and Mortimer in Pilkington's *Dictionary of Painters* (1810) attest that he did not share Blake's admiration for them. The three in no way constituted a school, but Blake was right, from his own perspective, in seeing all three as indicating a direction for his own artistic development. Fuseli, however, cannot be confined in his importance to influence and example. In addition to these, Fuseli provided sympathetic friendship, a commodity Blake was badly in need of throughout his career. Although we may now choose to regard Blake and Fuseli as contemporaries who shared similar interests, we must remember that for the young Blake Fuseli was a well-established artist of the older generation; he too was sixteen years older than Blake and had in 1780 returned from nearly a decade's residence on the Continent, mostly in Rome, where he had acquired a reputation for *terribilità* and unconventionality. They probably did not meet until around 1787; in 1788 Blake executed his first engraving after Fuseli, the frontispiece to Lavater's *Aphorisms on Man*, which Fuseli had translated into English. Here and in other engravings after Fuseli, Blake was allowed an unusual amount of freedom for an engraver working after another artist's conception, Fuseli leaving it to Blake to supply certain essential details.[19] This is also true of the engraving for Erasmus Darwin's *Botanic Garden*, 'The Fertilization of Egypt' (*Fig.* 2), executed in 1791, where Blake supplied among other things the sistrum to the left of Anubis. Fuseli's vocabulary of dramatic gesture, partially derived from the Mannerists, had an enormous impact upon Blake's style. The older painter's famous statement that Blake was damned good to steal from should be taken in the proper spirit,

as a graceful and witty compliment. Indeed, Blake so assimilated certain aspects of Fuseli's style that at times it is hard to tell conscious from unconscious imitation. (Is the sleeping figure in the *Jerusalem* title-page [*Pl.* 97] in the same position—reversed—as the one in Fuseli's *Nightmare* [1781] because Blake wanted to allude to this famous picture?) Fuseli's friendship and encouragement made him, for Blake, 'The only Man that e'er I knew/Who did not make me almost spew'.[20]

In addition to these older artists, there were two contemporaries with whom Blake formed important friendships at about this time: John Flaxman and Thomas Stothard. The friendship and artistic relationship with Flaxman lasted virtually all Blake's life (though with a distinct period of coldness in later

FIG. 2 *The Fertilization of Egypt*. 1791. Line engraving after Fuseli for *The Botanic Garden* by Erasmus Darwin. 7¾ × 5⅞ in. Cambridge University Library

years); the friendship with Stothard was terminated by the *Canterbury Pilgrims* affair of 1807 (see pp. 47–8), though Stothard was probably unaware that R. H. Cromek had in effect commissioned him to steal Blake's idea for a picture. Blake, Flaxman, and Stothard had a cross-fertilizing effect upon each other; and although in later years Blake would declare that the other two owed their reputation to him, we must not take this bitter retrospective view for the actual state of affairs in the 1780s. Flaxman was a brilliant designer whose conceptions cannot but have affected Blake. In particular, both were interested in developing a linear style of drawing derived from Greek vase-painting; this interest was to find expression during the next decade with the publication of Flaxman's designs for *The Odyssey* (1793), *The Iliad* (1793), and the tragedies of Aeschylus (1795), and in the eight plates Blake engraved for George Cumberland's *Thoughts on Outline* (1796). With Stothard Blake shared a pictorial vocabulary in which figures clad in a combination of leotard-like costumes and contemporary dress assume dance-like postures, often in pastoral settings. In the 1780s Blake executed numerous engravings after Stothard, including two productions of the short-lived partnership of Blake and Parker (*Zephirus and Flora* and *Callisto*, both 1784). The fact that the last of these is dated 1785 suggests an early deterioration of the relationship. The Farington Diary suggests, retrospectively, a cause. Fuseli told Farington on 24 June 1796 that Blake 'acknowledges the superiority of Fuseli: but thinks himself more able than Stothard'; while on 12 January 1797, 'Blake's eccentric designs were mentioned. Stothard supported his claims to Genius, but allowed He had been misled to extravagance in his art, & He knew by whom.' 'Many People', Blake later wrote, 'are so foolish [as] to think they can wound Mr Fuseli over my shoulder.' Stothard evidently envied Fuseli and, we may imagine, must have sensed and resented Blake's claim to superiority; thus the ground for the rupture between the two was prepared long before the affair of Cromek.

The 1780s were a particularly experimental decade for Blake, and we see him busy about many things, trying out various modes and media of expression. He could have poems printed in ordinary letterpress; he could illustrate his own manuscript poem; he could produce drawings and paintings without accompanying text; print relief-etched plates combining his poetry and designs; engrave after his own designs, and engrave after others. Of these activities, the first two proved of limited importance, while he continued the others throughout his creative life.

Poetical Sketches, printed for Blake's friends the Rev. A. S. and Mrs Mathew in 1783, contains no illustrations and for that very reason deserves mention here. With the exception of *The French Revolution* (1791), which exists only in a single set of proofs, Blake did not again have his poems printed in letterpress. There were several reasons for this, some of them economic— Blake, like Hogarth before him, was looking for a way to eliminate the middle man, and only by acting as his own publisher could he do this. However, an even more powerful reason was the polysemous nature of Blake's imagination. He needed to work in a mode in which text and design could be fruitfully and provocatively combined. Letterpress with engraved insets, in addition to being expensive, would still have lacked the fluidity of Blake's illuminated books, where even the calligraphy is part of the meaning and where each plate is a perceptual unit. By discovering his own particular process of relief etching, he enabled himself to do this.

According to John Thomas Smith, who alone of his biographers knew him at this early time, the discovery came to Blake in a vision of his brother Robert (who had died in February 1787):

his brother Robert stood before him in one of his visionary imaginations, and so decidedly directed him in the way in which he ought to proceed, that he immediately followed his advice, by writing his poetry, and drawing his marginal subjects of embellishments in outline upon the copper-plate with an impervious liquid, and then eating the plain parts or lights away with aquafortis considerably below them, so that the outlines were left as a stereotype. The plates in this state were then printed in any tint that he wished, to enable him or Mrs Blake to colour the marginal figures up by hand in imitation of drawings.[21]

Like many of Blake's visions, this one had a substantial basis. Blake had been thinking along these lines as early as 1784, when he wrote *An Island in the Moon.*

'—thus Illuminating the Manuscript.'

'Ay,' said she, 'that would be excellent.'

'Then,' said he, 'I would have all the writing Engraved instead of Printed, & at every other leaf a high finish'd print—all in three Volumes folio—& sell them a hundred pounds apiece. They would print off two thousand.'[22]

George Cumberland, too, was thinking of such a process in 1784, and communicated it in a letter to his brother Richard.[23] The process was simply an inversion of intaglio etching: the ridges of the acid-bitten plate were made to print rather than the valleys. The one precious fragment of a relief-etched plate in existence (from rejected plate *a* of *America*, now in the Lessing J. Rosenwald Collection, Library of Congress) permits a partial reconstruction of Blake's technique. 'The *America* fragment', writes Robert N. Essick,

> is etched to a depth of only .12 mm. on the average, and other evidence suggests that all of the relief etchings were given an extremely shallow bite. The striations around the relief plateaus indicate that Blake's acid was one of the so-called 'aqua fortis' mixtures described in early etching manuals. The *America* fragment also shows that Blake sometimes used step etching—that is, after a partial bite he would remove the acid and paint over letters or design elements with his acid resist, allowing it to flow over and beyond the original outlines. This procedure prevented underbiting by creating islands of protective resist around Blake's images.[24]

The one problem that remained for Blake to solve was how to reproduce the text—Cumberland's plan would have required the use of a mirror to enable the reader to read the reversed script. This would, however, have been a cumbersome operation. It has been suggested that Blake used a transfer method, laying a damp page of text over the copper plate and then removing it; this would leave the script in reverse on the copper plate, and after etching it would print the right way round.[25]

However, the relative crudeness of lettering in Blake's first relief-etched works—see, for example, *All Religions are One* (*Fig.* 3)—suggests that Blake learned, as many other engravers did, to write in a reversed hand and that it took him about a year to master the process fully.[26] John Linnell believed at one time that 'The most extraordinary facility seems to have been attained by Blake in writing backwards & that with a brush dipped in a glutinous liquid . . .'[27] Although the development of such techniques did not enrich Blake materially as Quid the Cynic had hoped, it did make him, in Gilchrist's words, 'literally the author of his own book'.

It was probably in 1788 that Blake published his first work in illuminated printing, *All Religions are One*.[28] (According to *The Ghost of Abel*, 1822, 'Blake's Original Stereotype was 1788.')[29] *All Religions* and two following tractates, both entitled *There is No Natural Religion* (*Fig.* 4), have as their subject the nature of human perception, Blake's argument being that all religious systems are constructs of the Imagination (here called 'Poetic Genius') and that therefore all of them are

FIG. 3
All Religions are One,
plate 2, title-page

symbols of the same essential truths. The designs as well as the verbal statements carry the argument forward. For example, in the upper part of plate 5 of *All Religions are One*, we see Eve being created from Adam's body (a

FIG. 3 (*cont.*) *All Religions are One*, plates 1, 3, 4, 5, 6, 7, 8, 9, 10. About 1788. Relief etching. Measurements vary from 2¼ × 1⅝ in. to 1¾ × 1⅝ in. San Marino, California, Henry E. Huntington Library and Art Gallery

FIG. 4 *There is No Natural Religion, b*, copy L, plates 1, 2, 3, 4, 8, 9, 10, 12. About 1788. Relief etching, some plates touched with water-colour. Measurements vary from 2⅜ × 1¾ in. to 2 × 1⅝ in. Reproduced from the facsimile published by the William Blake Trust

subject of perpetual interest to Blake; see below p. 63). What has this to do with the inscribed text 'As all men are alike in outward form, So (and with the same infinite variety) all are alike in the Poetic Genius'? Since man is created in God's image and woman also, being in Genesis a product of man's flesh, all human forms are images of the divine form; so the human imagination must also have the same essential structure. Such a design is not a mere adjunct to the text, nor does it make the same kind of conventionalized statement that the emblems in emblem books do. Blake is already at work creating the type of image that 'rouzes the faculties to act' (Letter to Dr Trusler, 1799).[30] He is also creating an iconic vocabulary which he will employ, with considerable enlargement and rich variation, for the next four decades. The vatic gesture of John the Baptist in plate 1 of *All Religions* reappears in plate 1 of *Visions of the Daughters of Albion* and in the 'Arlington Court Picture' (*Pl.* 89); the traveller with his staff in plate 7 of *All Religions*, in plate 14 of *Gates of Paradise* (*Fig.* 5), and in a *Night Thoughts* watercolour. The gestures of despair (hands to head, elbows out, *No Natural Religion b*, plate 8) and of triumph (arms extended horizontally, palms up, *No Natural Religion b*, plate 9) will be reiterated throughout Blake's works. Also, certain forms with symbolic significance are beginning to appear. The bearded patriarch, arms outstretched with palms downward in plate 4 of *All Religions* later becomes the sky-god Urizen. The use of the Gothic doorway in *No Natural Religion a*, plate 2 prefigures that in plate 1 of *Jerusalem*: through these portals we enter a lower world to redeem it by an act of imagination.

Having tested his mode of publication in the tractates, in 1789 Blake went on to produce his first mature work in illuminated printing, the *Songs of Innocence*, which to this day remains his best-known single work. The designs for *Innocence* have several types of component, often found together on the same plate. There are large illustrative units, much smaller but clearly definable images, and tiny border and interlinear images. The larger pictures sometimes literally depict the events in the poem, as in 'The Little Black Boy' (*Pl.* 7), where in plate 9 the Black Boy and his mother regard the sun while sitting in the shade of a tropical tree, and in plate 10 the Black Boy shields his English counterpart, who, under a willow, leans prayerfully upon 'our father's knee'. Even here there are some particularly Blakean touches: the shepherd-God is not the Father but the Son, and the idea of the Black Boy's superior tolerance for the beams of love is derived from Swedenborg's notion that the Africans were the remnant of the Most Ancient Church and therefore closer to God than the Europeans. These larger components of design are not always literally illustrative. In 'The Divine Image', for example, a great swirling vine or flame (the colouring differs in different copies), forming a reversed S with an added vertical tongue or filament rising from the first turning, unifies the page. At the base and top of this vine-like flame or flame-like vine are figures of the second type. At the bottom right Jesus creates Adam and Eve (who are, however, already separated by the vine-flame); at the top left a woman, perhaps embodying Mercy, Pity, Peace and Love, is directed by an angel towards two praying children. Botanical imagery is also present in the form of a leafy or flowering slender vine, which climbs up the much thicker vine-flame, signifying perhaps the omnipresence of Christ as the True Vine. In 'The Little Boy lost', a division of the plate into approximate halves also divides one type of imagery from another. In the upper half, the little boy pursues the 'vapour' or Will-o'-the-wisp, a symbol of the error of seeking a non-human god; below, six angels surround the text, indicating the continued presence of another reality. 'On Another's Sorrow' presents tiny figures of humans, birds, and plants, which, with a grapevine climbing the right side of the page and a Tree of Jesse climbing the left, create the visual meanings here without the use of large illustrative figures. As David V. Erdman has pointed out,[31] the visual elements of this page constitute a pictorial epitome of the *Songs*: appropriately, more copies of *Innocence* conclude with this plate than with any other.

Although many pictorial elements of *Innocence* could be singled out for closer attention, perhaps the images of trees and of tree-like vines are the most important. On the title-page a tree, which may represent knowledge, is entwined by a tender vine.[32] The frontispiece frames the figure of the Piper with relatively slender trees, a single one at his right and two gracefully, perhaps sensuously, intertwined ones at his left. A Tree of Jesse rises on both sides of the 'Introduction' plate, as Blunt observes,[33] with scenes related to the *Songs* placed in the oval panels. (Here is one of the few verifiable relationships between Blake's art and the art of the medieval manuscript—see Blunt, plates 16a and 16b). A vine-entwined tree gently shelters the Shepherd of plate 5. In the first plate of 'The Ecchoing Green', and again in 'Laughing Song' the central figures are sheltered by a sturdy oak—in the world of Experience this would be sinister, but in this unfallen world the oak is protective. In the second 'Ecchoing Green' plate two boys pluck grapes from a gigantic vine, one handing down a cluster to a girl below; in 'The Lamb' two delicate trees with their attendant vines arch to form a bower. But trees, even in Innocence, can be frightening. The Little Boy lost wanders beneath thick, leafless trees which remain sinister though impotent in plate 14 where the Saviour guides him, found, 'thro' the lonely dale'. A lion crouches at the foot of the tree in the first plate of 'Night', but an angel hovers just above him, and two more angels may be seen in the upper part of this tree and its attendant vine; in the second plate all three angels (more or less, depending on which copy is consulted) are visible along the tree trunk. 'The Little Girl Lost' (one of the original *Songs of Innocence*, later moved, with its sequel, to *Experience*) begins with a free-standing vine on the left and a beautiful willow accompanied by another vine above the lovers on the right; in the second plate, however, after the blight of sexual repression has struck, these are replaced by a thick dead tree on the left, and a live but even thicker oak on the right, with the lone figure of Lyca between them. On the same plate 'The Little Girl Found' begins: a lioness stands beneath another dead tree, but a vine at the left suggests that not all is lost. Turning the page, we find the vine has found a young tree to climb at the left, while the right is dominated by two enormous intertwined tree trunks, which recall the slenderer ones of the frontispiece and which seem related to the harmonious interplay of children and animals in the foreground. Innocence, as Northrop Frye pointed out long ago, is pastoral, Experience urban; in the *Songs of Innocence* we encounter, as we would expect, the tree and its frequent companion the vine as, most frequently, images suggestive of security, grace, and fruitfulness; but occasionally the tree can be of another sort, obscuring the way or barring it, and so adumbrating our wandering into another State.

In 1789 Blake also began to etch *The Book of Thel*, a composite work comprising eight pages. Describing the transition from Innocence to Experience, in this case an unsuccessful transition, *Thel* was probably not completed until about 1793.[34] Whether this means that Blake substituted a new ending for an earlier plate 6 we can only speculate. The title-page shows Thel as a shepherdess under a gently arching willow tree with its attendant vine (*Pl.* 6). Fascinated, she watches the Loves of the Plants as described by Erasmus Darwin, who personified the sexual lives of flowers in his *Botanic Garden* (1789). (This particular flower has been identified by Ruthven Todd as *anemone pulsatilla*, the pasque-flower.) The female who responds with fear and horror to the male's embrace is a miniature Thel, and her gesture foreshadows Thel's rejection of Experience at the end of the poem. In general, *Thel*, though a beautiful little book, lacks the richness of interest of the *Songs of Innocence*. The picture space tends to be set off sharply from the text, and the designs themselves, particularly those on plates 2, 4 and 5, are more or less illustrations rather than parallel statements. Exceptions are the slighter designs on plates 1 and 6. The first seems to

suggest alternative views of sex as either hostile (man pointing to eagle above T of title; armed warrior below and to the right of L) or fulfilling (man reclining on ear of wheat watching woman playing with child in the air below T). The small design at the end of the poem, a design Blake liked well enough to repeat reversed in plate 11 of *America*, shows three children riding the serpent of Experience; the eldest, a girl, guides the serpent with a rein as if to show Thel that it isn't so hard after all.

About 1789 Blake also produced a manuscript poem, *Tiriel*, accompanied by twelve illustrations. The poem was never quite finished, and we cannot tell in what medium Blake had intended to publish it. Presumably the designs would have been etched or engraved to accompany the text. Two of the designs stand out qualitatively above the rest, and it is notable that in both of these the design is not really an illustration of the text; it is as if even when illustrating his own verse Blake is fully at liberty only when the design introduces a new dimension of meaning. In no. 2, *Har and Heva Bathing* (*Pl.* 3), the aged couple are partially immersed in the waters of materialism, much like Urizen in plate 12 of *The Book of Urizen*, protected by their guardian Mnetha. Har and Heva's position is reminiscent of Barry's *Jupiter and Juno on Mount Ida*,[35] and Mnetha assumes the pose of a semi-recumbent river goddess. We could take this as a pastoral idyll did we not know from the poem that Har and Heva represent the arts in a state of debasement. Similarly, in no. 11, *Har and Heva Asleep*, the couple are covered by a beautiful floral quilt or counterpane. Once more, we would associate this with pastoral innocence if we did not know that

> . . . they were as the shadow of Har & as the years
>   forgotten.
> Playing with flowers & running after birds they
>   spent the day,
> And in the night like infants slept, delighted with
>   infant dreams.[36]

So there is just a hint in the text for the subject of no. 11, while the episode of no. 2 is not found in the text at all; but in both cases the meanings established in the text help us interpret the pictures, while the pictures bring in a dimension of meaning not found in the poem. Blake must have seen that this kind of cross-reference and enrichment of meaning could be accomplished with greater force through the composite art form that he had already employed than through entirely separated drawings and verse.

In 1780 Blake exhibited at a Royal Academy exhibition for the first time. His subject was *The Death of Earl Godwin*, illustrating the episode where the murderous Earl supposedly choked to death after swearing a false oath. (A sketch exists in the British Museum.) He had already executed one version of *The Penance of Jane Shore*, and was to repeat it in a more mature style about 1793 (*Pl.* 1). Among other historical works of this time are *The Making of Magna Carta, Lear and Cordelia*, and, slightly later, *The Ordeal of Queen Emma*. Blake's concerns in these early works are characteristic. Instead of portraying the history of England as a series of military triumphs, he chooses to emphasize such themes as divine intervention in human affairs (*Earl Godwin*), the hypocritical accusation of sin (*Jane Shore*), forgiveness of injuries (*Lear*), and the triumph of Liberty (*Magna Carta*).[37] The now lost early version of *The Bard, From Gray*, exhibited at the Royal Academy in 1785, introduces the motif of the poet as prophet. *Queen Emma* brings in the Blakean theme of accused Innocence triumphantly enduring. Related to these historical pictures are two more general in subject: *A Breach in a City, the Morning after the Battle* and *War unchained by an angel, Fire, Pestilence, and Famine Following*. The former shows the survivors mourning and searching among the dead, introducing a visual theme Blake was to use again on the title-page of *America* and in *Jerusalem*, plate 94, where women bend or lie prostrate over the corpses of their husbands. In the background of *A Breach*, a woman searches the fields of the dead in a pose foreshadowing that of the horrified mother in the 'Holy Thursday' of *Songs of Experience* (1793–4). A bird of prey like the one in *America*, plate 14, hovers at the upper left. Blake also did a larger version of this picture; and he also reworked the whole design in the frontispiece to *America*. The original *War* has not been traced; but

there are later versions of *A Breach in a City* in the Fogg Museum (*Pl.* 2) and elsewhere. These pictures have been taken to refer either to the invasion of France by Edward III or to the sufferings of the Britons after the Roman invasion, but there can be no doubt that Blake's almost obsessive interest in the subject was due to contemporary events. 'The American War began', he later wrote to John Flaxman. 'All its dark horrors passed before my face . . .'[38] As Gilchrist says, 'Companion subjects, their tacit moral—the supreme despicableness of war—was one of which the artist, in all his tenets thorough-going, was a fervent propagandist in days in which war was tyrannously in the ascendant.'[39]

Another area of virtually lifelong interest to Blake was the illustration of the Bible. For his first exhibited Bible pictures he chose the story of Joseph. In 1785 he showed at the Royal Academy *Joseph's Brethren Bowing Before Him, Joseph Ordering Simeon to Be Bound*, and *Joseph Making Himself Known to His Brethren*. He was undoubtedly familiar with the tradition by which Joseph was regarded as a type of Christ, and 'Joseph, an infant,/ . . . wrap'd in needle-work/ Of emblematic texture' does have this significance in *Milton* (24: 17–19).[40] But in these early Joseph pictures there is little symbolic meaning; instead Blake is concerned with rendering his subject in a frieze-like style and with establishing an 'Egyptian' atmosphere. The background of all three pictures is cut off abruptly to eliminate any sense of depth; the idealized figures, frequently in 'classical' profile, obviously owe much to Raphael and to Barry's Adelphi murals. The woman with the bowl held over her head in *Joseph's Brethren* and the curious screen composed of serpents and bulrushes in *Joseph Ordering* are clearly attempts to establish a feeling of locale. But the angel in the panel just over Joseph's head in *Joseph Ordering* is a particularly Blakean device, indicating the Divine Presence guiding Joseph. Another early Biblical illustration is the pen and wash drawing of *Job, his Wife and his Friends*, executed about 1785. Blake was to use this same composition as the basis for the tenth plate of his Job series in 1825, but once more we find no complex iconography in the early work. He had turned to the Bible as a subject in this early phase of his career, but he had not yet developed the method of interpretation by illustration that was to be, as it were, the signature of his mature method.

Two drawings after Shakespeare also belong to the mid-1780s. They are *Oberon, Titania and Puck with Fairies Dancing* (about 1785) and *Queen Katherine's Dream* (the earlier of the Fitzwilliam versions), probably made a year or two later. The former shows the influence of Fuseli and of Stothard, but does not succeed in drawing its various elements into a coherent whole, while the arbitrary placement of the smaller figures in the latter give it a cluttered feeling. (Blake was to rework the Queen Katherine subject at least three times, arranging the small figures in a swirling figure-of-eight pattern and so solving this particular problem.) In general, it must be said that none of these drawings, whether from history, from the Bible, or from Shakespeare, are great works of art. They are sometimes very dramatic in conception and moving in their conviction, but the figures tend to be flaccid when in motion and rigid when at rest. That the young Blake *could* draw well is attested by a pencil drawing in the British Museum which may have been done as an exercise for the life class at the Royal Academy. Whether or not this is a portrait of Robert Blake, as Sir Geoffrey Keynes suggests,[41] it is a fine academic nude, and the facial features are expressive yet subtle. Unfortunately, Blake did not consistently take such painstaking care in his early drawings, thus giving rise to an accusation that was forever to dog him: that his execution was not equal to his conception. However unfair this may be to the Blake of, say, *A Vision of the Last Judgment*, we must not be misled by the vehemence of his denial of this charge, at least not as far as these early works are concerned, especially when we remember that the works of the mid-1780s were produced by a man in his late twenties, not by an adolescent prodigy. Blake had already written great poetry, and in 1789 he produced his first great work of relief-etched composite art; but as Blunt puts it, 'As a painter, had he died at the age of thirty, he would hardly be remembered at all.'[42]

After leaving Basire's studio Blake, as we have seen, produced commercial engravings after Stothard, Morland, Cosway, Fuseli and other artists. Perhaps the best example of his commercial work of the 1780s is a scene from *The Beggar's Opera*, Act III, engraved after Hogarth and published by Alderman Boydell in 1788. But of far greater artistic importance than his reproductive works after others are the few engravings he produced after his own designs in the 1780s.[43] *Edward & Elenor* (Pl. 4), though bearing the date 1793, seems to be earlier in both design and theme, being closely related to *Jane Shore* and *Queen Emma*. Once more we see woman as a redemptive force in a threatening world, as Queen Elenor sucks the poison from Edward I's wound. It may be that the plate was executed in the 1780s but not used, for some reason, until 1793. The first state of the line engraving *Job* probably belongs to the middle or late 1780s. In 1793 Blake re-engraved the plate entirely, producing a stark, brooding effect, and added the inscription 'What is Man That thou shouldst try him every Moment? Job VII c 17 & 18 v'. Graphic works such as the print after Hogarth, *Edward & Elenor*, and the first state of *Job* show Blake as a competent working engraver whose technique was as yet not as advanced as his conceptions. His later re-engraving of some of his early works shows that he was himself aware of this; at the same time, his imaginative energy and force of conviction were already beginning to mark him as an artist of unusual power.

2. Thus Illuminating the Manuscript

LATE IN 1790 or early in 1791, Blake and his wife moved to Lambeth on the south side of the Thames. Here he completed *The Marriage of Heaven and Hell*, which was begun in 1790 but apparently not finished until 1793, wrote and published the *Songs of Experience* (1793–4), and produced the series of works now known as the Lambeth books, beginning with *Visions of the Daughters of Albion* and *America*, both dated 1793. In the middle of the decade he turned away from illuminated printing to produce his great series of colour-printed monotypes in 1795 and then to illustrate Young's *Night Thoughts* and the poems of Gray. Of course he continued other painting and engraving activities all the while—this was an extraordinarily fertile decade, even for Blake, terminating in 1800 with another removal, this time to the village of Felpham in Sussex.

The Marriage of Heaven and Hell is in part a satire on the writings of Emmanuel Swedenborg and on the New Jerusalem Church which Swedenborg's British followers had set up. William and Catherine Blake had been associated, if only briefly, with the Swedenborgians. They had attended the General Conference of the New Jerusalem Church in 1789 and had presumably assented to the 42 doctrinal propositions that had been unanimously endorsed there. Blake had read and annotated *Heaven and Its Wonders and Hell* (the English translation of 1784, probably read by Blake around 1787–8) and *The Wisdom of Angels Concerning Divine Love and Divine Wisdom* (translated in 1788 and probably read by Blake at about that time). His remarks on *Heaven and Hell* are sparse, but those on *Divine Love* are enthusiastic. 'Good & Evil are here both Good & the two contraries Married.'[1] Then, in his annotations to *The Wisdom of Angels Concerning Divine Providence*, published and probably annotated in 1790, Blake's attitude changes completely. **Now** Swedenborg is accused of being a 'Spiritual Predestinarian' as much as Calvin was or worse, a servant of 'Priestcraft' guilty of 'Cursed Folly!'[2] It must have been at about the same time that Blake conceived of a satire on Swedenborg's *Heaven and Hell* in which Swedenborg's Memorable Relations are

parodied by Blake's Memorable Fancies, presenting the Angels who instructed Swedenborg as insufferable stuffed shirts and the Devils in Hell as receptacles of life-giving energy. Blake had at first welcomed the idea of a New Church that would abolish the errors of the old ones, which inscribed over the door of its meeting-house the motto 'Now it is allowable' in contrast to the 'Thou Shalt Not' over the chapel in Blake's 'Garden of Love'. But as he read more of Swedenborg, he became convinced that 'Swedenborg has not written one new truth . . . he has written all the old falsehoods.'[3] As for the Swedenborgians themselves, they were behaving more and more like any other Church, at least in Blake's view. At the General Conference of 1790 a catechism for children was prepared, Joseph Proud's hymn-book was approved along with a form and order of worship, and the necessity of living according to the Ten Commandments was affirmed. At the next general conference (1791) ministers' garments were approved, and an attack was entered in the Minutes specifically against Thomas Paine and generally 'against all such principles of infidelity and democracy as were then circulating in this Country'.[4] As a result of a schism in 1789–90 on the subject of concubinage, those in favour of it were expelled from the New Church; these included, as it happened, the most active anti-slavery members. Although Swedenborg's own doctrine was by no means as harsh as Blake made out in the annotations to *Divine Providence*, he felt something of the anger of the disappointed convert. He therefore produced a book which would serve the double purpose of satirizing Swedenborgian doctrine and promulgating his own.

The title-page of *The Marriage* (*Pl.* 8) presents a graphic depiction of the marriage of contraries, as a naked figure from the clouds and another from the flames meet in a love-embrace. This theme of synthesis, as opposed to Swedenborg's static 'equilibrium', is carried forward throughout the text and designs. In general, the larger designs are rather closely related to the texts of the plates on which they appear, with the possible exceptions of plate 2, where the woman in a tree handing down fruit to another woman below has no clear relationship to 'The Argument',[5] plate 3 (in part), and plate 10. At the top of plate 3 a female figure bathes in flames as 'the Eternal Hell' revives thirty-three years after the Last Judgment that according to Swedenborg had taken place in 1757. At the bottom we see the birth of the 'new born terror' who will overthrow the 'starry king' of 'A Song of Liberty' (plate 25), while two lovers kiss in the midst of a balletic leap at the right. Plate 4 depicts in reverse the situation of the 1795 colour print entitled *The Good and Evil Angels* (*Pl.* 31), but 'The voice of the Devil' tells us that the bifurcation of Good and Evil is an error, that 'Energy, call'd Evil' is actually 'the only life' while 'Reason, call'd Good' is really 'the bound or outward circumference of Energy'. Here the 'Good' angel is protecting the child from the imagined threat of Energy, but the result of this may be seen in plate 5, as Satan falls. 'It indeed appear'd to Reason as if Desire was cast out; but the Devil's account is, that the Messiah fell, & formed a heaven of what he stole from the Abyss.' In the next large design, plate 10, a bat-winged devil impatiently shows two recording Angels a scroll—perhaps the 'Proverbs of Hell'—fresh from the Abyss.

The remaining seven major illustrations all clearly connect with texts on the same or neighbouring plates. The design on the top of plate 11 (*Pl.* 9) illustrates the genealogy of the gods in a spirit very similar to that of Wordsworth's famous *Excursion* passage published more than twenty years later, while at the bottom we see man floating passively away from the Jupiter Pluvius he has abstracted from himself. The argument of plate 14 is that 'the notion that man has a body distinct from his soul. Is to be expunged . . .' Blake's strategy for doing so is to employ the materials of his relief-etching process, 'printing in the infernal method by corrosives, which are salutary and medicinal, melting apparent surfaces away, and displaying the infinite which was hid'. The design shows the illusion of the body-soul dualism: the body, a grey corpse lying like a sepulchral effigy, the soul hovering above it in flames of energy. When perceived as one, they will fuse into the regenerate man of plate 21, who sits with the skull of the old Adam near his left knee and, in three copies, with the pyramid(s) of

Egyptian error behind him. (Blake repeats this image in plate 6 of *America* and in 'Death's Door' in Blair's *Grave*.) Two of the component forces of Blake's 'Printing house in Hell'—the serpent and the eagle—are shown in a synergic relationship, representing perhaps the collaboration of material knowledge and visionary wisdom. Plate 16 presents us with one of Blake's several versions of Dante's Ugolino: here the father and four sons are 'The Giants who formed this world into its sensual existence, and now seem to live in it in chains', but they are shortly to become representatives of the Prolific and the Devouring. A purposefully melodramatic Leviathan is pictured on plate 20, representing a Swedenborgian Angel's fearful view of the energies of revolution, but in plate 21 we see the regenerate man who will emerge from all this. The bestial Nebuchadnezzar, his contrary, appears on all fours in the last design (plate 24), a tyrannical king who believes in one law for the lion and the ox.

Described in this way, the designs for *The Marriage* seem very much like those of *Thel*, virtually illustrating the text and very much set off from it. This is indeed true of most of the large designs, but in *The Marriage* Blake also made exceptional use of interlinear illustrations, sometimes of such a tiny size that they can only be understood when magnified. He had used interlinear designs before and would again, but only in *The Marriage* do they carry a major burden of the meaning of the work. As David Erdman and his colleagues have shown, for example, the meaning of the Printing house in Hell (plate 15) is enlarged by a humanized burin on line 5; the archer and his apparent victim in plate 22 (just after the words 'A Memorable Fancy') represent Blake's conversion of the Swedenborgian angel by intellectual warfare; and the presence of a quincunx of birds frequently alludes to the five senses.[6] The presence of literally hundreds of such tiny images in *The Marriage* adds an entirely new dimension to the work, one which can only be explored in a detailed examination using enlargements of the plates. Why did Blake use this technique in such elaborated form only in *The Marriage*? He may have thought it particularly appropriate to this work, the subject of which is the hidden sources of knowledge, but even Blake cannot have been indifferent to the failure of these tiny images to communicate: a mode of representation that was not understood until 1973 cannot be considered a very successful one, however ingenious. Furthermore, painting the copies tended to obscure the minute details, so much so that the uncoloured copy B in the Bodleian shows them better than the coloured ones, while the John Camden Hotten facsimile of 1868, in which the facsimilist went over the fine details, is frequently a better guide to these images than are Blake's coloured originals.

On 10 October 1793, Blake issued an advertisement 'To the Public' listing ten works, engravings and illuminated books, for sale. Among these was 'Songs of Experience, in Illuminated Printing. Octavo, with 25 designs, price 5s.'[7] As we would expect, the landscape of Experience differs considerably from that of Innocence. Most conspicuously, the delicate trees and vines of the former give way to thick, leaflessly sterile trees in the latter, as in 'Holy Thursday', 'The Fly', 'The Angel', 'The Tyger', 'My Pretty Rose Tree', and 'A Poison Tree'. In the last of these, the Tree itself is the subject, representing a destructive process in the human psyche which Blake was later to render as the Tree of Mystery on which Christ was crucified. This Tree itself appears in the design for 'The Human Abstract', with the white-bearded figure who is elsewhere called Urizen knitting a snare below it. When the Innocence type of tree or vine does appear, it is in a context that gives it a parodic significance. In, for example, 'Earth's Answer', a large vine, usually bearing grapes, climbs up the left and over the top of the picture space; but beneath it is a vine-like serpent, spoiling this potential paradise. Large clusters of grapes hang conspicuously unharvested beside the door in 'Nurse's Song', while the little boy stands rigidly obedient, having his hair combed. The vine in 'A Little Girl Lost' has green leaves but no conspicuous grapes, and the tree it climbs is dead; the falsely promising leaves are on the same ironical level as 'the blossoms of my hoary hair' in Ona's father's fearful exclamation. There are grapes on the right-hand vine of 'The School Boy'—the vine at the left is dead—but this was originally a Song of Innocence, and at any rate the picture of three boys playing beneath the vine is

contrary to the text, where the Boy must 'sit in learning's bower' and 'buds are nip'd/And blossoms blown away'. No doubt this contrary relationship of text and design is what made the poem a good candidate for *Experience*. There is a fruitful tree in 'To Tirzah', but this plate was a later addition, first appearing in copy E of the combined *Songs* and expressing a spirituality not part of Blake's original conception.

Blake had learned the use of plant symbolism at least in part from Swedenborg, and although he may have rejected Swedenborg's doctrinal teachings by the time he etched *Experience*, he continued to employ his own version of Swedenborgian correspondences here and in other works. In *Heaven and Hell* Swedenborg writes:

> In general, a garden corresponds to the intelligence and wisdom of heaven; and for this reason heaven is called the Garden of God, and Paradise; and men call it the heavenly paradise. Trees, according to their species, correspond to the perceptions and knowledges of good and truth which are the source of intelligence and wisdom. For this reason the ancient people, who were acquainted with correspondences, held their sacred worship in groves; and for the same reason trees are mentioned in the Word, and heaven, the church, and man are compared to them; as the vine, the olive, the cedar, and others, and the good works done by men are compared to fruits. Also the food derived from trees, and more especially from the grain harvests of the field, corresponds to affections for good and truth, because these affections feed the spiritual life, as the food of the earth does the natural life; and bread from grain, in a general sense, because it is the food that specially sustains life, and because it stands for all food, corresponds to an affection for all good. (Note 111)

In a state of enlightenment, according to Swedenborg, the world becomes a garden to be enjoyed:

> By those who are intelligent gardens and parks full of trees and flowers of every kind are seen. The trees are planted in a most beautiful order combined to form arbours with arched approaches and encircling walks, all more beautiful than words can describe. There the intelligent walk and gather flowers and weave garlands

with which they adorn little children. Moreover, there are kinds of trees and flowers there that are never seen and cannot exist on earth. The trees bear fruits that are in accordance with the good of love in which the intelligent are. These things are seen by them because a garden or park and fruit trees and flowers correspond to intelligence and wisdom. (Note 176)

But in the fallen world, all things are changed into their hateful contraries. In 'The Garden of Love' we find a tombstone, two children praying beside a priest, and a briar-bound grave. Individual flowers, like the Sunflower and the Rose, each a hypostatization of an aspect of woman, are imprisoned in lives of either fruitless longing or secret and therefore tainted consummation. The destructive worm that destroys the life of the Sick Rose (see *Pl.* 11) is the obverse of the glorious flame-phallus of 'The Blossom' because the worm is 'invisible' and his love 'dark'. ('. . . Those who burn with vig'rous youth/', Blake wrote in his *Notebook*, 'Pluck fruits before the light.')[8] Only the lily, possessing neither thorn nor threat, embodies the immanence of love among the flowers of Experience.

In this second set of *Songs*, an alternative to the blasted landscape is the desolate cityscape. In the 'The Chimney Sweeper' we see the climbing boy with his bag of soot; in 'London' a boy leads an old man through the 'charter'd streets' of the city; another boy, or perhaps the same one, warms himself by a bonfire. The image of the city would always be a central one for Blake, and its meaning would not always be negative. On the contrary, for Blake the 'Spiritual Four-fold London' was to become the foundation of Golgonooza, the city of Art; and in *Jerusalem*, plate 84 we see the same child and the same old man ('London, blind & age-bent, begging thro' the Streets/ Of Babylon, led by a child'),[9] reversed, the child leading the old man past a church domed like St Paul's towards the true art and religion represented by the Gothic towers of Westminster Abbey. Context, we see again, is an important determining factor when we read Blake's designs.

The title-page of *Experience* emphasizes, appropriately, death and mourning, but the Innocent selves of the two mourners sport in the air above their heads. The frontispiece is more equivocal. We have the same two figures as in the frontispiece to *Innocence*, but the male has lost his pipe and the child has gained a pair of wings. The trees are leafy and a flock of sheep tranquilly browse. But the two main figures are no longer anchored by gazing at each other; instead, they are coming forward out of the picture space, making the transition, as Damon says, into the state of Experience.[10] The erstwhile piper has a firm grip on the hands of the child—perhaps it is necessary to carry his visionary burden like this in the world they are about to enter, but there is no danger that this winged joy will fly off. Is the youth a protective St Christopher or a jailer of inspiration? In the fallen world, is it necessary for him to be both? The vine beside the tree to the right is not the fruitful grape but the parasitic ivy.

Although Blake advertised *Songs of Experience* in the 1793 Prospectus, we do not know of any copies issued before 1794, nor do we know of any issued independently of the *Songs of Innocence*. There is every indication that once he had completed the second set of *Songs*, he regarded both as a single work, 'Shewing', in the words of his new subtitle, 'the Two Contrary States of the Human Soul'. For this combined work of 52 plates* he etched a new title-page, on which we see Adam and Eve, already wearing their girdles of fig-leaves, writhing in flames; at the upper right flies a bird, also dispossessed of Paradise.

The manner in which Blake coloured the *Songs* is typical of his procedure in colouring all the illuminated books, and as there are more copies of the *Songs* than of any other work, they provide valuable information about his colouring techniques. The early copies were painted in light watercolours. In some copies produced in the mid-1790s, at about the same time as Blake was

---

* Blake had advertised each set of *Songs* as having 25 designs. Since all the plates have some designs, either Blake executed two additional plates beyond the combined title-page or he intended to remove the two plates but thought better of it. ('To Tirzah', as previously mentioned, comes later, and another plate, 'A Divine Image', was etched but not included. Another rejected plate shows a nude female escorted through the air by five *putti*. A complete copy of the combined *Songs* had 54 plates [including 'To Tirzah'].)

executing his great series of colour-printed monotypes, colour printing was used; in the case of the combined *Songs*, this is true of copies F, G and H (in whole or in part). After this relatively short experimental period of colour printing, Blake returned to watercolour, sometimes working in delicate tones as before, sometimes in more opaque colours. (The tendency has been to assign the more crudely painted copies to Mrs Blake, but this results from a form of circular reasoning.) After 1800, Blake began using even richer colours in some copies, sometimes with gold leaf. Some very late copies are particularly rich in coloration. The general pattern, then, was from pale watercolours to (briefly) colour printing to very rich illumination. But having said this, we must immediately make some qualifications. First of all, Blake was at almost any time capable of returning to his early style of delicate watercolour. He also issued uncoloured copies from time to time. His general practice seems to have been to make up copies on order for a particular buyer, and his tendency to colour late copies of the illuminated books very richly

may have had less to do with his personal taste than with the preferences of his customers.

The Prospectus of 1793 also lists 'The Gates of Paradise, a small book of Engravings. Price 3s.' This series of 17 small engraved designs, comprising a little compendium of human experience, is the closest Blake ever came to producing a conventional emblem book (*Fig.* 5). Even here, however, the meanings are peculiarly Blakean rather than the conventional ones of emblem literature. The frontispiece, 'What is Man!', for example, employs the ancient idea found in the very name Psyche that Man is a larval form of being, and this theme recurs in Plate 6, 'At length for hatching ripe he breaks the shell' (cf. *Night Thoughts* I, 16). Plates 2–5 picture the four elements, which are also early representations of Blake's Four Zoas. Most of the emblems picture the vicissitudes of life in the world of Experience. Plate 1, 'I found him beneath a Tree', suggests Oedipal dependence; Plate 8, 'My Son! my Son!', Oedipal aggression. (The prototype of the latter as well as the source of the title is the story of

FIG. 5 *For Children: The Gates of Paradise*, copy B. 1793. Line engravings. Original leaves $5\frac{1}{4} \times 4\frac{1}{8}$ in. Plate measurements vary from $3\frac{1}{4} \times 2\frac{5}{8}$ in. to $2 \times 1\frac{3}{4}$ in. London, British Museum

Plate *a*, frontispiece

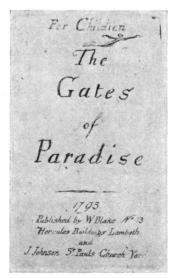

Plate *b*, title-page

Plate 1

FIG. 5 (cont.)
The Gates of Paradise,
plates 2 and 3

David and Absalom, which Blake also made the subject of a painting [*Pl.* 74].) In 7, 'Alas!' a youth pursues a flying joy with his hat. Blake describes himself as doing the same to a Fairy in *Europe*, but this fellow is more careless, having already killed one little figure. ('He who binds to himself a joy/ Does the winged life destroy'—*Notebook*.[11]) Plate 9, 'I want! I want!', with its debt to a cartoon by James Gillray,[12] links back to Proposition VI of *No Natural Religion b*: 'If any could desire what he is incapable of possessing, despair must be his eternal lot.'[13] In 10, 'Help! Help!', the overwhelmed self sinks in the sea of Time and Space; 'Aged Ignorance', 11, wears spectacles and has his eyes closed anyway; he cannot see the rising sun as his victim can. Plate 12 is another of Blake's treatments of the Ugolino theme, here seen as an accusation against the idea of divine retribution: 'Does thy God O Priest take such vengeance as this?' In 13 the series of vicissitudes is temporarily abandoned for a gleam of redemptive hope: 'Fear & Hope are—Vision'. This is in a sense a visual answer to the title-page of *Experience*, where the mourners bend over the rigid bodies of the dead; here the material body is still present, but a diaphanous spiritual body rises to astonish the mourners. (This will also be the theme of *The Death of the Good Old Man* for Blair's *Grave*.) In 14, 'The Traveller hasteth in the Evening', we see one of Blake's frequent depictions of a pilgrim with his hat and staff; a connection between this image and those in Stothard's designs for *The Pilgrim's Progress*, published in 1792, has been suggested.[14] In 15 we see to what the traveller has been hastening: 'Death's Door', an image to reappear in *America*, plate 12, in *Night Thoughts* (I, 6), and in Blair's *Grave*. Plate 16 shows the dead person wearing a shroud and still holding the now useless staff that

appeared in the two preceding emblems. The epigraph, 'I have said to the Worm: Thou art my mother & my sister', is from *Job*, and in the design the worm of mortality seems almost part of the dead human figure. Thus the series concludes with an image of death as imprisonment in the grave. As a whole, it is a congeries of loosely related thematic statements rather than a narrative sequence, and it is dark in effect, only two of the seventeen designs being hopeful.

In 1818 Blake returned to *The Gates of Paradise*. He reworked the engravings but did not add any from the store of sketches for the original *Gates* previously accumulated in his *Notebook*.[15] He also added to the captions of the emblems and wrote a poem, 'The Keys of the Gates', based on the emblems. Here, in accordance with his later thought, the emphasis is on regeneration, and seen in combination with the verses, the new *Gates* (*For the Sexes*) is considerably more optimistic than the original one (*For Children*). In a shorter poem added as an epilogue, 'To The Accuser who is The God of This World', Blake draws upon the concept of States, which is also typical of his later thought and has little to do with the original emblem series. This poem occupies a separate plate: the pilgrim-traveller lies asleep with his staff beside him; the bat-winged Satan of his dream, looking very much like the Spectre of Los in *Jerusalem*, plate 44, flies over him.

Visions of the Daughters of Albion was also advertised in the Prospectus of 1793. Consisting of eleven plates, in effect it is a sequel to *Thel*. Thel fled from Experience; Oothoon joyfully embraces it, only to be raped by a Urizen-surrogate, Bromion, and rejected by her lover, the aptly named Theotormon. The symbolism operates on several levels, a fact which will be increasingly true of Blake's illuminated works. The general theme is an

FIG. 5 (*cont.*)
The Gates of Paradise,
plates 4 and 5

attack upon the repressive institutions of society. Oothoon, the feminine Eros, is brutalized first by the puritanical Bromion, who afterwards condemns her as a harlot, then by the introspective Theotormon, who sits 'conversing with shadows dire'. In the social realm, the subject is slavery;[16] Bromion is the master of Oothoon's 'soft American plains', while Theotormon, whose conscience is that of a German Romantic Hamlet, merely listens to 'the voice of slaves beneath the sun, and children bought with money'. (One slave is pictured collapsed beside his pickaxe on plate 2.) There is a reflection here of the situation of Captain John Gabriel Stedman, who had gone to Surinam as a mercenary soldier, married a slave named Joanna, but found himself unable to purchase her freedom. Blake had recently illustrated Stedman's *Narrative*, and it is now known that the two became personally acquainted (see below, p. 38). More personally, the story of Oothoon and Bromion reflects that of Mary Wollstonecraft and her American lover Gilbert Imlay, with at least a possibility that Blake cast himself as Theotormon. This binding together of themes is characteristic of Blake's imagination. A century and a half later, Jean Genet was to make the connection between racial exploitation and sado-masochism the subject of *The Blacks*.

The perils of Oothoon are the subject of nine of the designs of *Visions*—ten, if we count plate 7, where one of four Daughters of Albion looks up at an Oothoon whose voice is heard in the text. In plate i (*Pl.* 12) she is chained back to back with Bromion while Theotormon huddles in despair; in ii (*Pl.* 10) she is pursued across the ocean by a flaming winged Bromion (see Notes to the Plates); in iii, she kisses a joy as it flies, having 'plucked Leutha's flower;' but at the bottom of 1 she lies on a cloud near Bromion, having been rent by

his terrible thunders. A female Prometheus, she is attacked by one of Theotormon's eagles on 3, to rise in a wave or flame over the oblivious Theotormon on 4, then collapsing in a heap, rejected, on 5. As Theotormon flagellates himself with remorse on 6, Oothoon weeps and turns away. She reappears among clouds in 8, arms outstretched and wrapped in flame: parodying the Bromion-figure of ii, she has become the Christ of the Parousia.

The illustrative technique of *Visions* is relatively simple, like that of *Thel*, with the designs relating, for the most part, to clearly identifiable passages in the text and, with minor exceptions in plates 2 and 5, occupying their own assigned space on the page. Still, the pictorial meanings are somewhat more challenging than those of *Thel*, that of the title-page most of all. In *Visions* we see Blake still trying to find a form adequate to the complexity of his vision. He was to find it shortly afterwards, with *America*.

1793 is also the date on the title-page of *America*, Blake's most complex illuminated work up to that point. The conception of such a book may have occurred as early as the watercolour *A Breach in a City*; there is also a drawing, identified by the inscription beginning 'Angels to be very small . . .', which, it has been suggested, is actually a sketch for the title-page of a poem called *The American War*.[17] In the British Museum Print Room there is another sketch for the title-page of *America*, which is much closer to the etched version. Both these sketches employ the figure of a woman crouched over the body of a man which first appears in *A Breach in a City*. There is also an ur-*America*, consisting of

FIG. 5 (cont.)
The Gates of Paradise,
plates 6, 7 and 8

at least three plates. The differences between rejected plate *a* and plate 3 are minimal: in the finished plate, a trumpeter still blows the flames of war in the middle of the pages, and the human family still escapes from those flames at the bottom left; at the top left soars Orc with broken chains, but his figure has been reversed, and the figure standing with a banner attached to a spear at the middle left of the proof (probably Albion's Angel armed) has been deleted in the final version. A comparison of plate 4 with rejected plate *b* shows still relatively minor differences in the designs. There are now two confounded fallen angels instead of one at the bottom right, and the rather slender tree further to the right in *b* has been transformed into the huge gnarled trunk of an oak tree (the patriotic song 'Hearts of Oak' with its naval associations had an especially ironical meaning to Blake). And now there appears in the foreground a killer whale or Orc, relating to the Pre-

ludium line 'I see a Whale in the South-sea, drinking my soul away'.[18] Albion's Angel in his grotesque dragon form still flies across the top of the page, while his aged human form, spear in hand, dives from the top left. The textual changes are much more extensive. In *b* Blake had named 'George the third . . . & his Lords & Commons'; this could have brought him to trial for sedition long before 1804. Also, the long description of king and council is Ossianic in the manner of *The French Revolution*; Blake replaced this bombastic passage with the genuinely powerful one in which Orc arises from the ocean 'a Human fire, fierce glowing, as the wedge/ Of iron heated in the furnace . . .' Only in the change from *c* to 5 has the design been entirely reworked. In *c* a man strangles a woman on a barren rock in the lower left; above, one naked youth averts his head in horror or despair and another flies downward with a trumpet. In plate 5 Blake has replaced this with an

interesting conception, taking the fallen Angel of plate 4 and hoisting him into the clouds on the back of a powerful muscular figure while two flying figures bear the scales and sword of Justice. Down falls the Angel on the left, while in the centre either he or his companion of plate 4 plummets into the coils of the Orc serpent. Flames of wrath come up from below. Some corrections written in pencil indicate that Blake at first intended merely to revise the again Ossianic text before deciding to replace it entirely.

We can see, then, that Blake went to unusual pains with *America*. The result was a work of greater power than any he had previously produced, and it may be that the fact that no copy exists with watermarks earlier than 1794 indicates that at least part of a year was needed before he was satisfied with what he had done. For a full discussion the reader must look to one of the detailed commentaries,[19] but we can at least indicate the various manners in which design and text relate to each other in this fully realized work of composite art. Simplest of all, no doubt, are those few designs that actually illustrate the text, as was the norm in the previous illuminated works; yet even here there are new elements of meaning. In plate 2, for example, the design clearly shows Orc getting free as described in line 2: 'The hairy shoulders rend the links; free are the wrists of fire . . .' Yet the design shows Orc emerging

from the *earth*, a detail not in the text (cf. *Gates of Paradise*, plate 3, where, however, the figure is completely inside the earth). Other visual elements not deriving from the text are the grapevine and the ear of wheat, associating this liberated aspect of Orc with Christ. Again, the design on plate 15 does show 'the fires of Orc/ . . . in wreaths of fierce desire,/ Leaving the females naked and glowing with the lusts of youth' (lines 20–2); it even shows the simile 'as a vine when the tender grape appears' (line 26); but the Daphne-figure at the middle left turns simile into metaphor: this female spirit is the vine itself. The plate is also particularly rich in interlinear pictures celebrating freedom.[20] So we see that even where text and design are closely related, in order to establish Blake's full meaning we need both.

At the other end of the spectrum are designs which do not emerge from the text of *America* at all. Sometimes a design will establish its own meaning, as with plates 4 and 5 already discussed. Also in this category are plates 7, 9, 11, 12, 13, and 14. Plate 1 and part of 13 are actually connected to passages in other illuminated books. The subject of plate 1 (*Pl.* 13) is the chaining of Orc by Los and Enitharmon, which occurs in *The Book of Urizen* (1794);[21] but the full aspect of the situation, including the horror of Los and Enitharmon at seeing Orc's chains become one with his flesh, were not to be

FIG. 5 (*cont.*)
The Gates of Paradise,
plates 9, 10, 11, 12 and 13

described verbally until *The Four Zoas*. (There is a separate plate, *The Chaining of Orc*, issued in 1812, demonstrating Blake's continued interest in this subject.) The top of plate 13 relates to a passage in *Visions* where 'The Eagles at her call descend & rend their bleeding prey'.[22] The lower part of the design, where the body of Man is preyed upon by serpents and fish, is a conception to which Blake was not to give verbal expression until *The Four Zoas*, Night IV. Plate 7 (*Pl.* 19) presents a situation that might be called contra-textual. The seven lines of poetry on this page convey the denunciation of Orc by Albion's Angel, to whom Orc is a 'Blasphemous Demon, Antichrist, hater of Dignities,/ Lover of wild rebellion and transgresser of God's Law'; but the design is a scene of Innocence— two children and a ram sleep under a graceful birch tree, on which sit three birds of paradise. Another bird of paradise flies upward; a grapevine springs up next to the tree. The contrast is very much that of the Leviathan episode in *The Marriage*, where 'All that we saw was owing to your metaphysics'.[23]

In plate 9 a germ of a suggestion may be provided by the line 'They cannot smite the wheat, nor quench the fatness of the earth', but the strange image of the child lying in a sea of wheat has a power of its own. It may be that the naked figure riding the swan on plate 11 is 'Boston's Angel', who 'cried aloud as they flew thro' the

dark night . . .' but this would not explain the choice of the swan (the soul, as in Shelley's 'My soul is an enchanted boat'?). The bottom design reverses that of *Thel*, plate 6. Both the bird and the serpent may be correspondences, for, according to Swedenborg, 'animals, according to their kinds and species, because they have life, are affections' (*Heaven and Hell*, Note 110). Plate 12 brings back the image of the old man entering 'Death's Door'; this time we must leaf back to 6 to find his regenerate self. In plate 14 a sibylline figure teaches an idolatrous youth the wrong kind of wisdom, as he leans on books and assumes a prayerful attitude (one of his brothers will escape to follow Jerusalem in *Jerusalem*, plate 4).

Sometimes the design may be, as it were, an extrapolation from the text, presenting readily identifiable figures but in such a way that their meanings are enriched and deepened. This is true of plates 8 and 10. In 8 we know that the white-bearded cruciform figure in the clouds is Urizen, although the speaker in the text is Orc. In 10 (*Pl.* 14) we see a cruciform naked Orc orchestrating the flames around him; once more, he is not named in the text but we recognize him as the 'Human fire' of plate 4. There is obviously a strong contrast here, between age and youth, clothed and naked, sky-god and fire-god. At the same time there is a comparison. Orc's expression is as doleful as Urizen's;

FIG. 5 (*cont.*)
The Gates of Paradise,
plates 14, 15 and 16

Orc's cruciform arms, like Urizen's, are palms-down, typically a gesture of repression unlike the palms-up position of the figure in the colour-printed drawing known as *Glad Day* (see below, p. 36). Orc here embodies what I have elsewhere called, borrowing a term from Camus, 'heroic fatality'.[24] He is sublime in his rebellion and yet at the same time ironically parodies the tyrant he has risen to overthrow. The richly evocative interplay of these two figures is yet another instance of how Blake's composite art can develop meanings which neither the verse alone nor the designs alone could have articulated.

The next illuminated book to be subtitled 'A Prophecy' was *Europe*, etched in 1794. (It was once common to call all of Blake's longer poems 'Prophetic Books', but we now see that Blake meant something more specific by the term: a book in which, as in the Old Testament, the divine pattern behind human history is discovered.) *Europe* continues the saga of revolution from the end of the American War to the beginning of the war against France in 1793; it also provides a mythological background, as in *America*, in the form of a Preludium. The frontispiece (*Pl.* 15) is perhaps Blake's best-known single work of graphic art. Also known as *The Ancient of Days*, it portrays God the Father as a powerful, Michelangelesque figure striking the circle of the world with a gigantic pair of compasses, himself a human compass as he leans down from his disc. The image derives from the Old Testament Proverbs and from *Paradise Lost* (see Notes to the Plates), but Blake has made a deliberate change of emphasis here. His Creator is the demiurge, and the grotesque left knee and impossibly elongated arm of this mighty form indicate Blake's ambivalence towards him. So do the surrounding ring of dark clouds, broken only in one place, and the beard and hair streaming in some wind between the worlds.

The graphic technique displayed in this plate, as may be seen in an uncoloured copy such as H, is extraordinary. The clouds are deeply textured by cross-hatching, while radiance streams from the solar orb in fine white lines to become lost in the blackness of the abyss. Blake colour-printed five of the twelve copies —B, C, D, E, F—in whole or in part, after painting

copy A for Isaac D'Israeli. He then reverted to water-colour for G and K. H and I were issued uncoloured. (L may be a posthumous copy, but in any event it was not coloured by Blake.) This variety of media gives us a good opportunity to compare Blake's various techniques: the relatively restrained colouring of A, the dense texture of the colour-printed copies, the austerity of the uncoloured copies, and the very rich coloration of K (Linnell-Fitzwilliam), characteristic of Blake's late productions.

The title-page of *Europe* shows the grinning, fork-tongued Orc serpent. Blake had at least four other conceptions for this page. One shows a naked male struggling with the serpent, one a bearded male riding on his back, one a muscular figure kneeling to him. (The first two are reproduced in *The Illuminated Blake*, 396–7; still another variant, 398, is slighter and need not concern us here.) The naked combatant is probably Los, who at the end of the poem 'call'd all his sons to the strife of blood'. The bearded rider is Urizen, complete with pen and tables of law, and his collaborative relationship with Orc here prefigures the unholy alliance the two will form in the latter part of *The Four Zoas*. The same is true of the kneeling figure, who looks very much like the worshipping Urizen of the frontispiece of *The Song of Los* (see *Pl.* 18). These variants are afterthoughts, with the new elements being drawn over the etched design; none of them are finished, and Blake did not re-etch the title-page. Nevertheless, the three major variants all show Blake's increasing disquietude about the principle of revolutionary energy represented by Orc, all suggesting the loss of the human aspect of revolution to the will-to-power.

Still vigorously experimenting with methods of conveying visual meaning, Blake included in *Europe* two full-page designs which have nothing at all to do with the literal details of the text, and yet belong to the world of deprivation and misery which is the subject of the entire work. These are plates 6 ('Famine') and 7 ('Plague', *Pl.* 16) both closely related to counterparts in the History of England series. Because of their free-standing nature, they tend to shift position in *Europe*, being either transposed or relocated in five of the original copies.

Europe also employs the mode of contrapuntal text-design relationships. Sometimes the meanings of the designs are explicit enough, as in plate 13, where a scaly jailor walks away from a chained prisoner, and in 2, where three figures enact the 'Devouring & devoured' vision of the 'Preludium', while a fourth turns away in horror. Other designs call upon only a moderate awareness of Blakean irony. The angels who stand beside the mailed warrior Rintrah in plate 5 are representatives of the old order; in 11 (*Pl.* 17) they cross fleur-de-lys staffs before a bat-winged Urizen enthroned as the Pope. Other designs are more enigmatic. On plate 9 two naked figures with curving trumpets make a magnificent baroque display, further emphasized by the great S-curve of grain across the page, reminiscent of 'The Blossom'. The beauty of the ogee curve, especially when enhanced by the beautiful green colouring of some copies, may seduce the viewer into a positive view of the scene; but actually these spirits are blowing blasts of disease upon the harvest, concomitant with the plagues that are referred to in the text (George Cumberland marked his copy 'Mildews blighting ears of Corn'). They can, at least temporarily, quench the fatness of the earth.

Another design that rouses the faculties to act is plate 8, where an old man makes an impotent protective gesture while a young woman clasps him for protection and huge clouds billow up behind them. Cumberland's inscription from Dryden's *Aeneid* again gives a clue: it is the fear of invasion that this Priam-figure helplessly tries to ward off. (The Troy-motif is continued in plate 15, where a family escapes from a burning city.) In 1, some knowledge of contemporary history is required: as Erdman has shown, the crouching assassin with the dagger is Edmund Burke, who had been caricatured by Gillray for his 'Dagger Scene' in Parliament, and the unsuspecting pilgrim wears the Foxite buff-and-blue.[25]

Some pages, as we would expect, present designs that do not connect with the text at any point but make their thematic statements independently. In plate 12 the oppression of the youth of England by Urizen and Enitharmon gives rise to a scene dominated by spider-webs and spiders, with one human victim at the lower right completely covered over with webbing. Plate 14 pullulates with forms of life which are in some way related to the pantheon of children upon whom Enitharmon calls, but it would be a mistake to link these creatures too literally with Manathu-Vorcyon, Leutha, Sotha, Thiralatha, and the others. Rather, we should perceive these images as projections of the vital forces of the children of Enitharmon, forces which may be creative or destructive and which are presented here in both aspects, but with the destructive aspect dominant. And so there are birds and butterflies, but the scene is dominated by caterpillars of the commonwealth, snails, and spiders. The three serpents at the bottom, however, do suggest the 'terrible Orc' of the last line of text, linking back with the grinning Orc serpent of the title-page and with the fiery-haloed one of plate 10. The latter presents a different aspect of Orc from the title-page: no longer ironic but wrathful, climbing up the page in seven loops, the world-week of history. (Here the text does present the same idea: 'Then was the serpent temple form'd, image of infinite/ Shut up in finite revolutions . . .') Orc's human form, however, is still present, unveiled by Enitharmon in plate 4, a design probably derived from a copy of Raphael's *Madonna del Diadema* (Louvre). The sleeping Orc has the flame-like halo that is transferred to the serpent of plate 10: Revolution maintains its alternative possibilities in *Europe*.

In *Europe*, Blake also maintains the complex relationship of design to text that he had developed in *America*. He continues to do this in *The Book of Urizen*, also published in 1794, which is at the same time the last really ambitious illuminated book of the Lambeth period. Consisting of 28 plates in a complete copy, *Urizen* is by far the longest illuminated book he produced (unless one were to count the combined *Songs*) before *Milton* (about 1809–10). Each of the seven extant copies has a different foliation. This is largely because of the inclusion of as many as ten full-page designs which could be shifted about without causing discontinuities in the text. The use of so many full-page designs is in itself remarkable. Magnificently colour-printed, they represent one of Blake's great achievements as a graphic artist, yet at the same time their beauty of colour and texture is indicative of the 'fallen' nature of his subject-matter. The intense coloration of rocks and flames, the blood-redness of the globe in plate 17 (*Pl.* 23)—these attractive elements are part of a mimetic strategy by means of which Blake renders Urizen's delusive world of matter in appropriate terms.

The chief participants in the drama of *Urizen* are Urizen, Los, Enitharmon and Orc, and one or more of them appears in at least 21 of the 28 designs. The title-page shows, as we would expect, Urizen himself, writing his books of law, a pen in one hand and a graver in the other; eyes closed, he seems to be tracing out the letters of a prototypical Law-book before him by feeling its surface with his foot. Behind him are the tables of Moses, shaped like a double tombstone; and above him is the barren Tree of Mystery. In plate 5, crowned with a fiery halo, the father-god opens the book to the reader: its colour-printed surface is beautiful, but the characters are illegible. The same white-bearded figure is wedged into rocks beneath the earth in plate 9; then in plate 12 he swims on his back in a pool of liquid, like Satan on the burning lake. He dives downward to explore his dens in plate 14; crouches manacled by Los in 22; and journeys through the created world with his globe of fire, watched by a lion, in 23. In 27 he rushes back away from the reader, and in 28 we find him enmeshed in his own Net of Religion (cf. 'The Human Abstract'). This white-bearded form of false wisdom is not, however, the only form Urizen can take. He can also appear as an athletic hero, cruciform in flames (but with palms down) in plate 3 or fallen down in despair in plate 4. In this manifestation, he much resembles his antagonist Los, and it is one of the ironies of *Urizen* that in some ways the two come to resemble each other. A third manifestation of Urizen is the skeleton of plates 8 and 11, for he must be bound by Los in order to assume even a quasi-human shape. Los himself first appears in plate 7, suffering the terrible effects of the fall, for as Blake was to put it when he came to write another version of this myth in *The Four Zoas*: 'he [Los] became what he beheld:/ He became what he was doing: he was himself transform'd.'[26] In both accounts the fall of Urizen precipitates the fall of Los. Los as imagination must create a body, an identity, for Urizen and his chaotic world; in doing so, the imagina-

tion becomes at least temporarily enslaved by the material reality which it has created. And so in plate 10 the powerful figure straining to lift a rock is not a back view of Urizen but the fallen Los, as a comparison with the title-page design of *The Book of Los* will confirm. In *Urizen* 11 (*Pl.* 22) Los lies collapsed, hammer in hand, beside the skeletal Urizen, whom he has manacled; a phallic tower is about to crash in flames between them. The ambiguity of the situation is that Los must chain Urizen in order to prevent a further fall into chaos, for the world without the order imagination imposes on it is, for Blake, barren. Yet the very act of circumscribing Urizen makes Los a prisoner in the world of limited perceptions he has created. In plate 16 Los is bathed in flames as Urizen was in water, knees drawn up like a foetus, powerful arms helpless behind his head. In 18 he rises in the flames, holding his hammer, but in 19 he hunches over in despair as Enitharmon, his now-separate emanation, flees from him 'In perverse and cruel delight'. The family group is completed by the birth of Orc, born in flames in 20. All three are the subject of plate 21 (*Pl.* 24): Orc, about to endure Oedipal exposure on a mountain-top, embraces his mother while Los, the Chain of Jealousy growing from his body, looks on. Los is now bearded and is beginning to look like the patriarch he has chained, just as his sexually possessive Chain of Jealousy is ironically similar to Urizen's repressive Net of Religion. The effects of the fall govern even the Eternal Prophet.

In *America* and in *Europe* Blake had created a historical myth which described, taken as a whole, the events of eighteen hundred years of history. *Urizen* supplies a myth at the same time psychological and cosmogonic, describing how humanity got into the state of bound perception and material being. In 1795 this myth was to be amplified in *The Book of Los*, while *The Song of Los* and *The Book of Ahania* would bring psychological, cosmogonic and historical events together.

The Song of Los (1795) is a beautiful little book, but represents a decline in ambition from the three peak works of the Lambeth period, consisting of only eight plates and extant in only five copies. The arrangement is virtually symmetrical. The textual part consists of two sections, headed respectively 'Africa' and 'Asia', consisting of two plates each. These are separated by a full-page design (*Pl.* 20), known in a separate water-colour as 'Oberon and Titania' (*Pl.* 21). There is also a full-page frontispiece (*Pl.* 18), followed by the title-page, and a full-page tail-piece. All plates are relief-etched and colour-printed, showing extraordinary effects of mottled colours which Blake also achieved in his monotypes of 1795. In the frontispiece a gowned figure (probably Urizen, the primeval priest) worships an occulted sun, a sphere with dark, fibrous texture—the colour-printing is especially effective in giving a textured effect—also suggestive of a fertilized ovum. The world of *The Song of Los* is subject to the combined powers of the forces of generation and Urizenic law. Then, in the desolate landscape of the title-page, we see 'Noah, as white as snow,/ On the mountains of Ararat';[27] the skull on which his left hand rests may be that of 'Adam, a mouldering skeleton'. The patriarch looks up to the sky as if seeking hope but finding none; in the text of 'Africa' Adam and Noah watch Urizen give his constrictive legal dispensations to mankind 'By the hands of the children of Los'—i.e., imagination does the work of repressive reason, delivering myths which become Law. Plate 3 presents a pre-lapsarian pastoral scene reminiscent of *America*, plate 7, but the huge serpent looping among the letters of the title 'Africa' foreshadows what is to come. Next we see Har and Heva (cf. *Tiriel*) fleeing as a winged form escapes to the right. Then plate 5 takes us into a fairy world: Titania sleeps in one lily while Oberon keeps watch, against a starry sky, in another. The scene is beautiful, but deceptively so, for Blake's fairies are no friends to man. At best they are neutral, controlling our generative powers. They can be put to human use, as the speaker of *Europe* does when he catches the Fairy or as in the similar situation of the MS. poem 'The Marriage Ring'. But they can also be the agency of cruel, un-satisfied desire. The scene itself foreshadows the level of existence Blake was later to call Beulah: a sweet and pleasant rest from the labours of Eternity, which becomes a trap if one tries to linger in it too long.

'Asia' opens with two lovers hidden in a cave or recess under the title, the youth trying to revive the maiden; a giant figure crouches helplessly at the lower right, and on the right of the next plate a naked figure falls headlong. The tail-piece is more optimistic: Los, a combination of Thor, Hephaistos, and the alchemical Vulcan, rests after having created the sun, an event which actually occurs in *The Book of Los* (1795) and which is also pictured there in plate 5 but far less powerfully. *The Book of Los* represents an even more modest attempt than *The Song* and comprises only five plates. The great wave of energy that had produced the Lambeth books was ebbing, and as if in recognition of this, Blake abandoned his relief etching in *The Book of Los* and *The Book of Ahania* (also published in 1795 and consisting of only five plates). These were produced by conventional intaglio etching, though *The Book of Los* is colour-printed. Both these books are closely related in subject to *The Book of Urizen*. *The Book of Los* goes over the creation-as-fall myth again, this time from Los's point of view. *Ahania* continues the story of Urizen with the struggle of Urizen's son Fuzon against the primeval father. No doubt this material was intended for a *Second Book of Urizen*, but Blake, seeing how slight *Ahania* was in comparison with its predecessor, decided to obliterate the *First* from the title of the earlier book instead.

The Book of Los begins with a frontispiece depicting Eno, the aged earth-mother, who speaks in the first page of text. Hunched over in a cave, she expresses in her doleful countenance the pain of fallen existence. The title-page shows Los in the same predicament as in *Urizen*, plate 10, wedged in among rocks. Plate 3 pre-sents a strangely ingenious design where the *O* of *LOS* in the title becomes an egg, in which sits the white-bearded Urizen, wearing the papal tiara and holding his book of Law. All around and below him spreads the Web of Religion, and a naked man and woman struggle to be free of it. The diminutive figure over 'Chap. 1' is reading a book, whether Urizen's or *The Book of Los* itself we do not know. *Ahania* has even fewer designs and is coloured in watercolours. The frontispiece (*Pl.* 25) shows a grotesquely huge Urizen pawing Ahania; on the title-page she flies through the sky lamenting (cf. *Urizen*, plate 13). After three pages of undecorated text in which the unsuccessful revolt of Fuzon takes place, a tail-piece pictures the mangled leavings of the guillotine. Only one complete copy each of *Ahania* and of *The Book of Los* are known to exist.

Why did Blake abandon the mode of the illuminated book in 1795? We have seen that in the space of about seven years he had developed a form which was capable of making artistic statements of great complexity and of equally great beauty. Yet he was not to complete a new illuminated book for fourteen or fifteen years. Part of the immediate answer may be simply that his artistic energy was finding other outlets in print-making and in painting. Yet the answer cannot be so simple, for we know from *The Four Zoas* MS. that in the late 1790s and early 1800s he remained preoccupied with the myth he had evolved in the Lambeth books and that his intention, never completely realized, was to create a single mythopoeic work that would incorporate, elaborate and extend the material of the earlier prophecies. Part of the reason for his seeking other means of expression was no doubt simple self-preservation. After the State Trials of 1794, there was a general retreat on the part of radicals, and Blake must have been aware that there were certain risks attendant on prophecy. In 1795

Richard Brothers, the self-styled Prince of the Hebrews who had in 1794 published two books of prophecies denouncing war and empire, was arrested. According to *The Times* for 6 March 1795, the charge against him was grounded on a statute from the reign of Elizabeth; Brothers was accused of 'Unlawfully, maliciously, and wickedly writing, publishing, and printing various fantastical prophecies, with intent to cause dissension and other disturbances within the realm . . .' Brothers was examined by the Privy Council and consigned to an asylum for the insane, where he spent the next eleven years. Blake, aware that he himself was mocked with aspersions of madness, must have found the event cautionary. Three years later, annotating Bishop Watson's *Apology for the Bible*, he bitterly wrote 'To defend the Bible in this year 1798 would cost a man his life.'[28] Defending Tom Paine against the Bishop, Blake also says: 'Paine has not attacked Christianity. Watson has defended Antichrist.' But 'I have been commanded from Hell not to print this, as it is what our enemies wish.' The world was not to have the Bible of Hell after all—at least not for the time being.

3. Ruind in His Ruind World

MEANWHILE, IN THE MID-1790s, Blake was becoming increasingly interested in colour-printing. As we have already seen, the illuminated books of this period tend to be colour-printed, but in 1795 or so he began to issue separate colour prints, mostly taken from the illuminated books. Blake knew that in doing so he was tearing the designs out of their context of meaning. Two of these groups of prints, now known simply as *A Small Book of Designs* and *A Large Book of Designs* (British Museum), were executed for the miniaturist Ozias Humphrey, and many years later Blake wrote: 'Those I Printed for Mr Humphry are a selection from the different Books of such as could be Printed without the Writing, tho' to the Loss of some of the best things. For they when Printed perfect accompany Poetical Personifications & Acts, without which Poems they never could have been Executed.' (To Dawson Turner, 9 June 1818.)[1] But not all these colour prints were *disjecta membra* of the works of composite art. Three of the prints in *A Large Book of Designs* were probably never associated with any illuminated book. *Joseph of Arimathea Preaching to the Inhabitants of Britain*, closely related in theme to the History of England series, shows the preserver of divine vision as a bearded, bard-like figure, dramatically dressed in white, in contrast to the rich colours worn by his listeners; he gestures prophetically with one outstretched hand while in the other he holds the staff that sprouted into a flowering thorn-tree at Glastonbury. There are two examples of this print but only one known state. Also colour-printed from a copper plate is *Our End is come* (*Pl.* 27), but this had been published in 1793 as an uncoloured line-engraving in two states, the second of them inscribed with two lines from Blake's 'Prologue, intended for a Dramatic Piece of King Edward the Fourth'. The horrified king and warriors whose end has come are closely related to the tyrant figures of the writings and drawings of the Lambeth period, especially to *America*, from which the original title derives.[2] Later, perhaps about 1803, Blake was to rework the plate and issue the uncoloured line-engraving once more, this time with the engraved inscription 'The Accusers of/ Theft Adultery Murder' and the caption at the bottom 'A Scene in the Last Judgment/ Satan's holy Trinity The Accuser The Judge & The Executioner'. Once more, as in the case of *Joseph of Arimathea among The Rocks of Albion*, Blake took up an early engraving in order to rework it in his more mature engraving style and at the same time to give it a symbolic significance characteristic of his later thought. The third colour print in *A Large Book of Designs* not taken from any illuminated book is perhaps Blake's most famous separate plate. Known from a sentence in Gilchrist as *Glad Day*, this colour-printed monotype, executed about 1794, actually has no original title. It depicts the naked male figure as a sublime human form, cruciform with palms up—the gesture of total giving—against a glorious sunburst, which creates the effect of a halo. He stands in a balletic posture on a richly coloured mound of earth. The source for Blake's pencil drawing of this figure, as Blunt has shown, is a bronze statuette of a faun, engraved in *De' Bronzi di Herculano*.[3] Later Blake reworked the same copper plate once more for an uncoloured line-engraving (*Pl.* 43). The date on this engraving is somewhat misleading, and it should be noted that the inscription reads 'WB inv. 1780'—*not* 'WB inv. & sculp'. 1780 probably refers to the pencil drawing (Victoria and Albert Museum); the line engraving may be dated 1800–3. The two lines of verse below the latter support this later date: 'Albion rose from where he labour'd at the Mill with Slaves:/ Giving himself for the Nations he danc'd the dance of Eternal Death.'[4] This theme of heroic self-sacrifice does not become a central one in Blake's work until after 1800.

In issuing his colour-printed relief etchings independent of text, Blake had, perhaps unwittingly at first, hit upon a new major medium of expression. It is true, as he later said, that the illuminated books could only be 'Printed perfect' with the text included. But what about designs conceived as symbolic statements independent of any text, as was apparently the case with the three prints just discussed? Here lay a new field for the energies diverted from illuminated printing. Also, for such colour-printed monotypes Blake found he did not need to go through the troublesome and time-consuming procedure of engraving copper plates or of relief etching them with his step-biting process. If only two or three examples of each print were to be produced, he could paint them in tempera on millboard, take prints while the paint was still wet, and finish the prints with watercolour and pen. According to Butlin, he did not repaint the millboard after taking each impression, so that the first impressions generally would be the strongest and the closest to Blake's original conception, while each subsequent impression was weaker and required more finishing-up.[5] This process clearly did not lend itself to the kind of mass production Blake had once envisaged for the illuminated books: he was now seeking fit audience though few. There are twelve of these colour-printed drawings in all, none known to exist in more than three impressions. The emphasis, like that in the illuminated books of the 1790s, is on the fallen world: only three of the twelve are in any way optimistic, the remaining nine depicting in various ways the anguish of material existence.

Six of the twelve colour prints are Biblical in subject, though, as we would expect, they render their subjects in a Blakean perspective. *Elohim Creating Adam* (Pl. 28) is an example of this. For Blake the creation of Adam's material body is a catastrophe; Elohim (who will become the third Eye of God in *The Four Zoas*) is a blind demiurge whose fingers grope the face of an Adam wound round with the worm of mortality. This negative view of the Old Testament's God is continued in *God Judging Adam* (formerly thought to be 'Elijah in the Fiery Chariot'[6]), where God is a Urizen-figure who condemns the creature made in his own image. *Nebuchadnezzar* (Pl. 29) elaborates the conception of *The Marriage*, plate 24 (reversed): the tyrant figure becomes the *reductio ad absurdum* of power, a taloned beast crawling among massive, contorted trees. The reason for the choice of *Lamech and His Two Wives* is puzzling, both because of the obscurity of the subject and the peculiar treatment of the two wives, who are seen almost as if growing into each other. However, Blake may have been influenced by the significance Sweden-

borg attaches to Lamech: 'That by Lamech is signified vastation, may appear from the following verses [Genesis 4] 23, 24: where it is said, that he slew a man to his wounding, and a little child to the blackness of his wound; where by a man is meant faith, and by a little child, charity' (*Heavenly Arcana*, Note 406). A note of hope is struck in *Naomi Entreating Ruth and Orpah to return to the Land of Moab*. Blake had a special sympathy for the outsiders and the transgressors of the Bible (Ruth appears in his genealogy of Mary in *Jerusalem*, plate 62, as do Lamech's two wives); Naomi's compassion towards the Moabite Ruth is no doubt what interested him in this subject. With *Satan Exulting Over Eve*, however, we are back quite literally in the world of the Fall. Satan appears in two forms: as bat-winged 'hero' armed with spear and shield hovering over the recumbent naked Eve, and as crested serpent twined about her body (Blake was to use a variation on this powerful design in his *Paradise Lost* illustrations). The only New Testament subject is *Christ Appearing*. Despite the interest of the design itself, the perpendicular figure of Christ rising over the bowed apostles (a conception related to Blake's undated early drawing *The Good Farmer*), it must be said that this picture is notably lacking in power and that Blake at this point was more successful in conveying the demonic than the beatific.

The six non-Biblical colour prints include several of Blake's greatest artistic achievements. *Newton* (Pl. 30), shows the essential form of this 'mighty Spirit . . . from the land of Albion,/ Nam'd Newton' (*Europe*)[7] as a mighty Michelangelesque figure, but like his compass-wielding counterpart, the Ancient of Days, he is muscular to the point of being grotesque. His thorax is too long for the rest of his body and its reticulations suggest the carapace of a beetle; in posture he is mid-way between the hunched-over Adam and the on-all-fours Nebuchadnezzar. He is drawing a diagram from the *Opticks* under water, as the streaming sea-anemones to his left attest. The lichened rock behind him is beautiful, but in the way that the world of Blake's colour-printing can be beautiful—that is to say, it is a seductive and deadly beauty. There is no such ambiguity in *The House of Death* (Pl. 33). Deriving from a passage in *Paradise Lost* (XI, 477–93), this picture shows the Lazar-house as

Michael describes it to Adam. Five of the 'numbers of all diseas'd' are seen, three lying on a woven straw mat of a type Blake frequently uses for those in an abject state. The figure at the right is despair, his head shaved like a lunatic's, who 'Tended the sick busiest from Couch to Couch'; Blake has introduced the dagger or flaying knife in his left hand. This figure will recur as Skofield in *Jerusalem*, plate 51. Death, white-bearded and blind, presides over the scene, his darts emanating from a scroll of curses unrolled before him. Blake had done a drawing with the same title a few years before, but the colour print is a far more powerful design; Fuseli's drawing of the same Miltonic subject (1791–3) depicts furious external action, while the power of Blake's conception is in its magnificent tautness. *Hecate* (*Pl.* 26) derives from Virgil's characterization of the triple Hecate in the *Aeneid*, a copy of which Blake owned in Dryden's translation. If Nebuchadnezzar represents debased power and Newton debased reason, Hecate represents debased sexuality. She appears to have borrowed one of Urizen's books, but none of her three heads is reading it. The creatures around her are so grotesque as to border on the humorous.

The two remaining colour prints are drawn from Shakespeare and from Blake himself. *Pity* employs a device Blake frequently uses in illustrating the works of other poets: the literalization of a trope. Where Shakespeare in *Macbeth* says 'pity, *like* a naked new-born babe,/ Striding the blast' (emphasis mine), Blake depicts an actual naked babe in the air, received into the hands of one of 'heaven's cherubin, hors'd/ Upon the sightless couriers of the air'—and we know the horses are 'sightless' because their eyes are closed! The dead woman on the ground may represent the 'horrid deed'—in *Macbeth*, the murder of Duncan. *Pity* introduces another gleam of grace into the nightmare world of the colour prints, but it requires a murder to produce it. Unlike *The House of Death*, this invention is not entirely successful, for the parts do not cohere. Shakespeare made the two clauses parallel; it is Blake who makes the 'cherubin' receive the 'new-born babe', yet no symbolic meaning emerges from this. Last, Blake's own *Good and Evil Angels* (*Pl.* 31) elaborates the design on plate 4 of *The Marriage*, reversed. There, however,

the 'evil' of the Evil Angel was only apparent, for on the same plate we are told that Energy, though 'call'd Evil' is in reality 'the only life'. In the colour print the figure in flame seems to have become really evil, with his sightless eyes and over-muscled limbs. Blake's attitude towards Orc having become more ambivalent, he has made the incarnation of Energy slightly disturbing, and the 'Good' angel's gesture may be genuinely protective. Perhaps this is the one colour print that should still have been 'Printed perfect' with accompanying text.

One further remark should be made about the colour prints: they are, for Blake, relatively large works. *Newton*, for example, measures $18\frac{1}{8} \times 23\frac{5}{8}$ in., and this is a fairly typical size. Blake was used to working in a comparatively small space, and the size of these twelve pictures contributes a great deal to their monumentality. So, of course, does their technique. As Butlin says, 'These represent the culmination, both artistic and technical, of Blake's development of colour printing in the first half of the 1790s.'[8]

By the middle 1790s Blake had not achieved any remarkable success as a professional engraver. He had executed plates for a number of books, mostly published by the radical bookseller Joseph Johnson, and in some instances he was also the designer (six plates for Mary Wollstonecraft's *Original Stories from Real Life*, 1791, 1796; five plates for Erasmus Darwin's *Botanic Garden*, 1791–5). His most ambitious project to date had been sixteen engravings after John Gabriel Stedman's illustrations for Stedman's *Narrative of a Five Years' Expedition Against the Revolted Negroes of Surinam*, engraved in 1792–3 and published in 1795. This was obviously more than a mere commercial job for Blake; his powerful engravings emphasize the brutal degradation of colonialism and slavery, and in the course of the work he and Stedman became friends. (We now know, thanks to Stedman's diary, that Blake was 'mobb'd and robb'd' in 1795; we wish we knew more.) All this, however, did not add up to the kind of career Blake had envisaged. The designs for the *Narrative* were not his own, and he was only one of several engravers employed on the project. Then in 1795 his fortunes seemed about to change. Richard Edwards, a bookseller in Pall Mall, commissioned him to draw and engrave the designs for a folio edition of Edward Young's *Night Thoughts on Life, Death and Immortality*. This enterprise looked very promising: it was an era of great projects of book illustration, Boydell's Shakespeare Gallery being the greatest of all of them, and Young was a popular poet whose works had never been issued in such a luxurious edition. Blake set about his work with characteristic energy, producing 537 watercolour designs, of which 43 were engraved for Edwards's edition of the first four Nights published in 1797. This was to be followed by the next five Nights, but no further instalment appeared. In 1799 Blake wrote bitterly to George Cumberland: 'For as to Engraving, in which art I cannot reproach myself with any neglect, yet I am laid by in a corner as if I did not Exist, & Since my Young's Night Thoughts have been publish'd, Even Johnson & Fuseli have discarded my Graver.'[9] Despite the commercial failure of the 1797 *Night Thoughts*, the watercolour series contains some of Blake's most striking and most interesting designs, as well as (inevitably in the case of so many drawings produced at such speed) a number of clumsy and dull ones. The engravings, though they are not examples of Blake's fully mature technique, constitute a major contribution to the art of the illustrated book.

There are three distinctive aspects of the *Night Thoughts* series, one having to do with design, the other two with content. Physically, the drawings present a unique appearance: pages from the first editions of the individual Nights (published [for R. Dodsley] from 1742 to 1745) were inlaid on the drawing paper, and Blake drew in the border areas surrounding the printed text. This same procedure was followed in the edition of 1797, with the new letterpress substituted for the Dodsley text. 'The engravings', says Edwards's prospectus, 'are in a perfectly new style of decoration, surrounding the text which they are designed to elucidate.' We do not know certainly that this perfectly new style was Blake's idea, but it seems likely that it was, for it uses the printed page in a way very much like his manner of using the pages in the illuminated books. There is, of course, a considerable loss of fluidity, for there could be no interlinear designs and the border

figures could not invade the text as they frequently do in the illuminated books. In compensation, Blake worked in terms of the page as a whole, making ingenious use of the block of text sometimes as a divider, sometimes as an incidental barrier behind which the picture subject may be imagined to continue. His approach to Young's poem was in a way similar to his approach to the Bible in the Lambeth books. The text was not a fixity to be illustrated in its own terms but rather raw material with an underlying meaning which the artist would bring out. Sometimes this would indeed result in a design close to the text, sometimes in an ironical inversion of meaning, sometimes in the literalization of a trope. Also, Blake allowed the symbolic figures of his illuminated books to emerge in his designs for Young, and in many ways we can also see the elaboration of symbolism that was to occur in *The Four Zoas* anticipated in the watercolours and engravings for *Night Thoughts*.

In a way, the illustrations to *Night Thoughts* are meant for the ideal student of Blake, one familiar with his symbolic conceptions and with his habits of thought. But many of the designs make their point without such specialized knowledge. It would be an insensitive viewer who did not perceive the irony of watercolour 81 (Night III, page 6), ostensibly illustrating 'Where *Sense* runs Savage, broke from *Reason's* chain,/ And sings false Peace, till smother'd by the Pall'. The beautiful, exultant naked woman about to be entrapped in the cloak of a white-haired flying figure is an emanation falling into the destructive toils of Urizen; but we do not need to know this in order to sense that the effect of the picture is different from that of the passage. At other times the meaning of a picture may appear plain, as is the case with the striking title-page of Night the Eighth, watercolour 345 (*Pl.* 35), which is clearly an apocalyptic vision of the Whore of Babylon and the seven-headed Beast, but which has a complex symbolic significance that Blake was to elaborate later (see Notes to the Plates). Similarly, the extraordinarily powerful depiction of Narcissa in the title-page to Night the Third, watercolour 78 (*Pl.* 36) uses Young's text only as a springboard to a Blakean meaning: there are two conceptions of timelessness, one as cyclical recurrence and one as a breaking-through to Eternity. These are represented by, respectively, the resplendent Orc serpent and the white, radiant female figure whose arms reach upward with a sweep reinforced by the rest of her body. The literalized trope may also have an extended symbolic meaning. In the design engraved on p. 23 of the 1797 edition (*Pl.* 38), a father with either an exceptionally large hand or an exceptionally small baby takes the measure of the infant, ostensibly illustrating 'We censure nature for a span too short'. To Blake measuring with a span means imposing limits, as the God of the Old Testament 'Who hath measured the waters in the hollow of his hand, and meted out heaven with the span . . .' (Isa. 40: 12). This child, like the child of 'Infant Sorrow', who is described as 'Struggling in my father's hands', is being initiated into a constricted reality. He is also like the child Orc in *Urizen*, who is treated similarly by Los: 'In his hands he siez'd the infant,/ He bathed him in springs of sorrow'.[10] Another seemingly straightforward situation is that engraved on p. 35 (*Pl.* 39): 'Teaching, we learn'; but the teacher is Urizen, imparting the wisdom of number, weight, and measure to his all-too-willing pupils. At the right sits Vala, in an interesting pre-Art Nouveau chair that grows out of a plant; she is enfolding a child in her seemingly protective garment. Above her, an Eternal on a cloud watches with amusement, and on the top of the page another plays the harp. This picture does have an accessible surface meaning, but even the doughtiest reader of the 1797 text must have realized that engraved p. 12 (*Pl.* 37) has nothing to do with the marked line 'Its favours here are trials, not rewards'. The anonymous 'Explanation' of the engravings, attributed to Henry Fuseli, is not much help: 'The frailty of the blessings of this life demonstrated, by a representation in which the happiness of a little family is suddenly destroyed by the accident of the husband's death from the bite of a serpent.' The meaning here depends on symbolism which Blake himself had not yet fully elaborated elsewhere (see Notes to the Plates). Such pictures as these have, in the words of the *Descriptive Catalogue*, 'mythological and recondite meaning, where more is meant than meets the eye'.[11]

Of course not all of Blake's designs for *Night Thoughts* have a mythological and recondite meaning. Nor do all of them have as their emphasis the negative implications of life on earth. The engraved frontispiece for Night the Fourth, for example, depicts a radiant, risen Christ—athletic in the manner of Michelangelo's drawings of the Resurrection, with which Blake would have been familiar, and flanked by two Flaxmanesque angels, one of whom holds the cast-aside cerement. One could find many passages in Blake's works to accompany this design, but one needs none. The engraving of Christ with pierced hands and feet, wearing the crown of thorns, is less successful, but also needs no particular Blakean explanation. Just as the quality of the designs in this series varies immensely, so also does the degree of literalness and the degree of optimism or pessimism present. Nevertheless, two qualified generalizations may be made. First, the *Night Thoughts* series is Blake's first extensive essay at illustrating the works of a modern poet so as to create a parallel pictorial work, one which may at times contradict, invert, or undermine the manifest meaning of the text. Second, despite a number of significant exceptions, the focus of the *Night Thoughts* series is on the nature of life in the fallen world. By far the majority of the *Night Thoughts* drawings dwell on this theme, and, more important, most of the truly memorable ones do so. Still, the direction of Blake's later interests is emerging, as we see in watercolour 264. This Christ, perhaps Blake's most persuasively authentic in feeling so far, emerges cruciform, palms (bearing stigmata) up, from a well of deep darkness. His radiance pierces the darkness of the tomb and makes the dead dimly visible. But the radiance is still ultimately dissipated in darkness, and only half of Christ's emerging body is visible. As Jean Hagstrum writes, 'Though transfiguration is not complete, it is being achieved.'[12]

Blake executed one more extensive series of designs for an eighteenth-century poet in the 1790s. In 1798[13] John Flaxman commissioned him to illustrate the poems of Thomas Gray as a present for Flaxman's wife Anna. The method chosen was similar to that for the *Night Thoughts* watercolours: the letterpress text was inlaid on sheets of Whatman drawing paper and the poems surrounded by the designs, numbering 116 in all. In theory the result should have surpassed the Young series. Gray, like Young, has a richly pictorial style, giving Blake ample choice of subject-matter, and Gray is by far the finer poet. Also, Blake had a strong interest, independent of commissions, in Gray's poem 'The Bard'. He had already exhibited a picture on this subject in 1785 and would again in 1809; there are also two powerful pencil sketches for the latter (*Pl.* 51). Furthermore, Blake obviously derived some of his later symbolism from 'The Fatal Sisters' and 'The Triumphs of Owen'. Nevertheless, the illustrations have a cumbersome, even slapdash quality, possibly due to the haste with which they were executed. Another reason may be Blake's lack of sympathy with some of the subjects, as is all too evident in the illustrations to the 'Ode on a Distant Prospect of Eton College' and the 'Elegy Written in a Country Church-Yard'. Gray's nostalgia simply was not a congenial attitude for Blake, yet at the same time he apparently felt constrained to remain closer to the manifest content of the poems than he had in the case of Young. Perhaps design 42, in 'The Progress of Poesy' but not directly related to it, is a form of revenge. The poet sits pensively immersed in his book, oblivious to the beautiful cherub and the St John figure (a true poet, who looks up, pen in hand, from his opened scroll to regard the cherub) in the Gothic window behind him. The only completely successful set of designs to Gray comprises the six drawings for 'Ode on the Death of a Favourite Cat Drowned in a Tub of Gold Fishes'. Here Blake succeeds both in capturing the wit of Gray's poem and in creating a myth of his own, whereby the cat Selima becomes a representation of the soul forced by 'Malignant Fate' (*Pl.* 40) into the world of Generation.[14]

In the later 1790s Blake also continued to produce single works, though his output of these was necessarily diminished by the extensive Young and Gray projects. One of the most interesting of these individual works is *Malevolence* (1799; *Pl.* 41) both in its own right and because it prompted Blake to the first written defence of his art. The drawing was commissioned by the Reverend John Trusler, author of *The Way to Be Rich and Respectable*. In the picture as described by Blake, 'A Father, taking leave of his Wife & Child, Is watch'd by Two Fiends incarnate, with intention that when his back is turned they will murder the mother & her

infant.'[15] Dr Trusler was not pleased with the picture and his criticisms of it elicited a defence of visionary art from Blake in a letter dated 23 August 1799.[16] The purpose of his art, Blake says, is to involve the imagination of the spectator. 'The wisest of the Ancients consider'd what is not too Explicit as the fittest for Instruction, because it rouzes the faculties to act.' The proportions of Blake's figures are those of 'Michael Angelo, Rafael & the Antique, & of the best living Models'. There follows an eloquent defence of the Imagination, in many ways foreshadowing the more extensive comments Blake was to make in his prose writings of about 1805–10:

And I know that This World Is a World of imagination & Vision. I see Every thing I paint In This World, but Every body does not see alike. To the Eyes of a Miser a Guinea is more beautiful than the Sun, & a bag worn with the use of Money has more beautiful proportions than a Vine filled with Grapes. The tree which moves some to tears of joy is in the Eyes of others only a Green thing that stands in the way. Some See Nature all Ridicule & Deformity, & by these I shall not regulate my proportions; & Some Scarce see Nature at all. But to the Eyes of the Man of Imagination, Nature is Imagination itself. As a man is, So he Sees. As the Eye is formed, such are its Powers. You certainly Mistake, when you say that the Visions of Fancy are not to be found in This World. To Me This World is all One continued Vision of Fancy or Imagination, & I feel Flatter'd when I am told so. What is it sets Homer, Virgil & Milton in so high a rank of Art? Why is the Bible more Entertaining & Instructive than any other book? Is it not because they are addressed to the Imagination, which is Spiritual Sensation, & but mediately to the Understanding or Reason? Such is True Painting, and such was alone valued by the Greeks & the best modern Artists.

Notice that this is not mere subjectivism. We all see according to what we are, but this does not mean that we perceive with equal truth. Our State, as Blake would soon call it, determines the extent to which we can perceive the truth, which is assumed to be one and imperishable, although manifesting itself to us according to our capacity to receive it. Dr Trusler did not dislike *Malevolence* because of any real faults in the picture; it was because he had 'fall'n out with the Spiritual World'.

Trusler's attack stung Blake but did not cause him serious concern; in addition to his own confidence in his art, he had just found, as he wrote to George Cumberland on 26 August 1799, an 'employer' who had given him 'an order for Fifty small Pictures at One Guinea each'.[17] This employer was Thomas Butts, a chief clerk in the office of the Commissary General of Musters, and the order was for fifty tempera pictures illustrating the Bible, now known as the Butts Series. Although executed from 1799 to 1800, these were but the first group of a very large number of Bible illustrations that Butts purchased from Blake over the course of the next decade, and for our purposes they are best discussed together at a later point after we have followed Blake through the next phase of his career.

4. My Three Years Slumber on the Banks of the Ocean

ON THE NIGHT OF 18 September 1800, William and Catherine Blake, with their material belongings in sixteen boxes and portfolios, arrived in the village of Felpham in Sussex. The move had been arranged by William Hayley, to whom Blake had been introduced through their mutual friend Flaxman, and for whom he had already executed three engravings illustrating Hayley's verse *Essay on Sculpture*. The immediate object of the move was to provide Blake with work, beginning with engravings for Hayley's work in progress, *The Life and Posthumous Writings, of William Cowper, Esqr*. 'I intend that this very amiable Man', Hayley wrote to Cowper's cousin, Lady Harriet Hesketh, 'shall execute, under my own Inspection, all the plates for the Work; & am persuaded he will produce a Head of Cowper, that will surprise and delight you . . .' (25 February 1801).[1] Lady Hesketh had disliked the original Romney portrait, which had attempted to capture the gleam of inspiration in the poet's eye. (In this, as in many things, Lady Hesketh had an independent opinion, for the portrait had been a favourite of Cowper's.) She was finally reconciled, however, to the fine engraving Blake produced after Romney for volume I of Hayley's *Life*. He produced six plates in all for the finished work, and his role in working with Hayley was very close: 'The warm-hearted indefatigable Blake', Hayley wrote to The Reverend John Johnson, 'works daily by my side, on the intended decorations of our Biography' (1 October 1801).[2] The benevolent Hayley found other work for Blake to do. Among other things, he commissioned him to draw eighteen heads of poets to decorate his library. Blake can have had little interest in some of these, such as Voltaire, Cicero, Dryden, Pope, and Klopstock; but others—Spenser (*Pl.* 70), Shakespeare, Milton (*Pl.* 69), and Cowper—do reflect genuine interests of his own. Hayley also wrote, for the benefit of the Blakes, a series of ballads about animals, for which Blake designed and engraved illustrations. These were first published singly, the copper plates being passed through the Blakes' own rolling press, and were hawked about among Hayley's friends; they were then

published as a volume with fourteen plates in Chichester in 1802 and again in London (but with only five plates) in 1805. It must be said that Hayley's insipid verse seems to have contaminated Blake's pictorial style: 'The Horse' (*Fig.* 6) is a fair example of the stagey, mannered nature of these illustrations. Hayley also tried to obtain commissions for Blake from his friends, and

FIG. 6 'The Horse', from Hayley's *Ballads*. 1805. Line engraving. 4¼ × 2¾ in. Harvard University, Houghton Library

as a result Blake painted a number of miniatures but, according to Gilchrist, drew the line at painting a set of hand-screens for Lady Bathurst.[3]

Despite all initial sanguinary optimism about the move to Felpham, Blake began to suspect more and more strongly that his art was being reduced to mechanics and triviality. He could engrave pictures of animals for the *Ballads* and draw Tasso for Hayley's Library; he could paint portrait miniatures, but he could not find encouragement for his highest aspirations. 'I find on all hands', he wrote to Thomas Butts, 'great objections to my doing any thing but the meer drudgery of business, & intimations that if I do not confine myself to this, I shall not live . . .' (10 January 1802).[4]

Opinion has been divided as to Blake's judgment of Hayley. In earlier days there was a tendency to see Hayley through Blake's eyes as a trivial, obtuse man who had entertained an angel unawares. But, after all, when Blake was arrested for sedition in 1803, Hayley behaved handsomely towards him; and some of Blake's *Notebook* verses about Hayley cannot be endorsed by any reasonable person. It is hard to believe that Hayley, 'when he could not act upon my wife/ Hired a Villain to bereave my Life' (the second line coming, strangely enough, from Blake's early poem 'Fair Elenor').[5] Morchard Bishop's delightful biography *Blake's Hayley* (London, 1951) provides a valuable corrective to Blake's biased view of his would-be benefactor. Yet there still remains something strange about Hayley's motivation. 'The truth is', Blake wrote to his brother James, 'As a Poet he is frighten'd at me & as a Painter his views and mine are opposite; he thinks to turn me into a Portrait Painter as he did Poor Romney' (30 January 1803).[6] It is interesting that Romney's son held very similar views. According to the Rev. John Romney, he wrote the *Memoirs of the Life and Works of George Romney* (London, 1830) in order to correct misrepresentations about his father made in Hayley's *Life of George Romney* (London, 1809): 'Mr Hayley's friendship was grounded on selfishness, and the means by which he maintained it was flattery.' Hayley persuaded Romney not to exhibit in order to be admitted to the Royal Academy 'assigning as his motive the *mental peculiarities* of his friend' (pp. 139–40). Indeed,

John Romney's image of Hayley and his 'canting hypocrisy' is very similar to Blake's portrayal of him as Satan in *Milton*: 'with incomparable mildness,/ His primitive tyrannical attempts on Los, with most endearing love/ He soft intreated Los to give him Palamabron's station'.[7] Satan-Hayley has only the Science of Pity, being unaware of the unconscious destructive envy he feels towards the artist he thinks he is befriending.

During the Felpham period Blake engraved little that was not connected with Hayley's projects. He also found it hard to execute more Bible illustrations for Thomas Butts. In a letter dated 11 September 1801,[8] Blake apologizes for 'my seeming neglect of your most pleasant orders'; on 22 November 1802, he writes that he fears Butts is with some reason offended with him.[9] In the summer of 1803, however, he sent Butts seven watercolours. The next Butts account is dated January 1805,[10] placing the great majority of the Butts Bible pictures after Felpham (see below, pp. 56–8). Blake did, however, make progress on 'a Sublime Allegory, which is now perfectly completed into a Grand Poem'.[11] There are only two extant candidates for this work—*The Four Zoas* and *Milton*. The former was almost certainly begun before Blake came to Felpham and finished after his return to London; the latter bears the date 1804 on its title-page but could not have been published before 1809–10. On the whole, *The Four Zoas* is the likelier possibility. 'This Poem', says Blake to Thomas Butts, 'shall, by Divine Assistance, be progressively Printed & Ornamented with Prints & given to the Public.'[12] Although it really would have required divine assistance to etch the huge *Four Zoas* in copper plate, he may have had in mind a reduction of the manuscript to a more realistic size. Certainly the MS. was begun as a holograph adorned with drawings, but by July 1803, when the letter to Butts was written, Blake had made so many revisions that he could no doubt think of it as preliminary to an illuminated book. *Milton*, on the other hand, seems to be referred to in a previous letter to Butts (25 April 1803).

Had it been finished as Blake had originally intended, *The Four Zoas* manuscript would have been a beautiful composite work, written out in elegant copperplate hand and illuminated with watercolours. However, the poem was abandoned rather than concluded, and the designs are in a much more fragmentary state than the text. Only those on pages 3, 4, and 5, all in pencil, ink, and wash, are relatively finished. Page 3 depicts a reclining female figure, the 'Aged Mother' whose 'Song . . . shook the heavens with wrath'.[13] Page 4 shows a winged Eros riding an explicitly phallic serpent and taking aim with a bow and arrow, a reference to the theme of Blake's second subtitle, 'The torments of Love and Jealousy'. The despairing winged figure on p. 5, very similar to the one on the frontispiece of *America*, is identified by Damon as the Spectre of Tharmas, described on the following page as 'a shadowy human form winged'.[14] The rest of the drawings vary from fairly well worked-up ones to the merest of sketches. Sometimes we find it possible to identify a subject from the *Four Zoas* text or from other works by Blake. For example, the drawing on p. 74 is Urizen with his globe of light, referred to in the text of p. 74 and shown similarly in *Urizen*, plate 23. The family triad on p. 60, as the text indicates, is made up of Orc, Enitharmon, and the jealous Los, a subject Blake treated somewhat differently in plate 21 of *Urizen*. Page 62 shows the aftermath of the chaining of Orc in a manner similar to that in *America*, plate 1, and the separate plate of 1812. Plate 87 of *Jerusalem* will present a variation of the drawing on *The Four Zoas*, p. 9, where the blind Enion vainly pursues her terrible children Los and Enitharmon. The nude woman on her knees on p. 86 (*Pl.* 42) with her hands on her prominent breasts must be the triumphant Vala, and the quarrelling nude couple on p. 112 must be Los and Enitharmon, enjoying their perverse and cruel delights. Thus the reader familiar with the poem of *The Four Zoas* and with Blake's illuminated works can explicate the subjects of some of the drawings. This is not true in numerous cases, however, and the meaning of many of the drawings has remained a matter for speculation. This is in part due to the unfinished nature of some of the drawings, while some of the most finished drawings are almost certainly studies for other works. The Christ of p.116 is clearly related to *Night Thoughts* drawings 107 and 108, preliminary to the 'Christian Triumph' engraving. The figure studies on p. 66 and the androgynous nude on p. 76 are evidently not related to any passage or episode in *The Four Zoas*. Furthermore, even if the *Four Zoas* drawings themselves were completely finished, it is unlikely that some of them would lose their enigmatic character. As Bentley says, 'At first the drawings tend towards a literal pictorial representation of the text, while those added later are less directly related to the poem, more suggestive, perhaps, of parallel or slightly divergent ideas . . . The *Vala* drawings seem to reveal Blake's changing concept of the relation of the illustrations to the text in his Prophecies.'[15]

One further aspect of the *Four Zoas* drawings is worth mentioning here. On a number of pages, Blake drew winged phalluses, some of which have been rubbed away (perhaps by a later hand), while others remain on pp. 42, 100, and 134. Blake evidently got the idea for these from both the text and the illustrations of Richard Payne Knight's *An Account of the Remains of Priapus . . . A Discourse on the Worship of Priapus* (London, 1786). Knight had discovered a remnant of Priapic worship at Isernia, near Naples, in 1781, and he published his findings with speculations about their meaning as a letter addressed to Sir William Hamilton. In ancient painting and sculpture, according to Knight, 'the organ of generation represented the generative or creative attribute' (p. 27). Blake took over this symbolism in *Vala* but gave it a decidedly more negative twist of meaning in accordance with the 'torments of Love and Jealousy' theme. He seems to have been particularly influenced in this respect by a half-page engraving of phallic objects in Knight, fig. 2, showing a flying phallus, and by fig. 4 of plate 5, showing a phallic snake. It would of course have been difficult to publish such illustrations in Blake's time—Knight had had the first edition of his book recalled on the advice of friends—but the single copy of *Vala* was intended for a limited audience.

5. In the Caverns of the Grave

THE BLAKES returned to London in September 1803 and took a house in South Molton Street, near Bond Street, where they were to live for the next eighteen years. For a time Blake busied himself with errands associated with Hayley's *Life of George Romney*, tracking down the widely dispersed paintings so that they could be engraved, but when the book appeared in 1809 it contained only one engraving by Blake himself. Casting about for new commissions, he obtained one through his friend Flaxman, and engraved Flaxman's drawing of a newly discovered statue of Ceres for Prince Hoare's *Academic Correspondence* of 1803. He began to paint Bible illustrations with renewed energy for Thomas Butts. He also engraved three plates for Flaxman's *Iliad* in 1805 and re-engraved five of his own designs for Hayley's *Ballads*, published by Richard Phillips that same year. What we know of Blake for the two years following his return to London indicates that he was actively pursuing his art and trade but that he had no major project on hand other than the Bible illustrations for Butts. This was suddenly to change in September 1805 with the appearance in Blake's life of Robert Hartley Cromek.

Cromek was an engraver whom ill-health had forced into entrepreneurship and publishing. A friend of Flaxman's, he came to Blake with a proposal for an illustrated edition of Robert Blair's celebrated poem, *The Grave*. Blake was to produce first forty, then twenty designs, from which he would engrave fifteen illustrations. He would receive only one guinea per design but would realize his profit from the payments for the engravings. Blake seems to have worked very quickly on the designs, drawing to an unusual extent, even for him, on his repertoire of past works. In November a prospectus was issued, advertising fifteen prints 'from designs invented and to be engraved by *William Blake*'. But then something strange happened. A new prospectus, also dated November, was published, according to which the book would contain 'twelve very spirited engravings by *Lewis Schiavonetti*, from designs invented by *William Blake*'.[1] Blake had lost his commission to a successful imitator of Bartolozzi. We can only speculate as to the reason, but we do know that Cromek had announced that 'The original drawings, and a Specimen of the Stile of Engraving' could be seen at his place of business on Warren Street. It seems likely that Blake produced his relief-etched print of *Death's Door* (*Pl.* 45) for the occasion, and that some of Cromek's customers took fright at the deliberately archaic ruggedness of the style. A comparison with Schiavonetti's published engraving (*Pl.* 46) shows what swayed Cromek's mind: Schiavonetti is a competent stipple engraver who takes no risks and produces a smooth, rounded and somewhat bland effect. Paradoxically, it may have been Schiavonetti's very competence that caused the criticism that Blake's designs were materially absurd, such as Robert Hunt's objection that 'The greatest poets have failed in their attempts "to connect the visible and invisible worlds", [the expression is from Fuseli's introduction] and have conveyed no just idea of the incomprehensible and intellectual faculty, whenever they have tried to embody it.'[2] Precisely because Blake's graphic style is at this point non-realistic (the same feeling of archaism comes through in the full-page etchings for *Milton*), his attempt to connect the visible and invisible worlds would have been more likely than Schiavonetti's to effect that willing suspension of disbelief which constitutes poetic faith. Blake had to endure not only the loss of the income he had expected but hostile reviews from the *Examiner* and the *Anti-Jacobin Review*; only the *Monthly Review* published a mildly favourable notice. Yet *The Grave* was through much of the nineteenth century the work for which Blake was best known. Thanks to Cromek's industry in obtaining endorsements from thirteen Royal Academicians and in selling at least 684 copies by subscription, the 1808 *Grave* was a publishing success—though not, of course, for Blake.

The published designs for *The Grave*, even through the mediation of Schiavonetti's system, are powerful in their simplicity. The busyness of some of the *Night Thoughts* illustrations is absent, and instead Blake has assimilated diverse elements of his art into unified visual expression. The engraved title-page, *The Skeleton Reanimated*, is a sort of Blakean signature piece; the portrayal of *The Counsellor, King, Mother, & Child in the Tomb* brings back the love of Gothic architecture and tomb effigies that Blake had acquired in Westminster Abbey. *The Soul exploring the recesses of the Grave* has a particular meaning for Blake that is not present in Blair—indeed, this scene itself does not occur in Blair's poem. In *The Four Zoas* 'the Caverns of the Grave & places of Human Seed' refers to the seminal vesicles and ovarian tubes, dark passages that lead the generated soul downwards. This same imagery occurs in a more extensively developed way in *The Descent of Man into the Vale of Death*, but this descent is towards not eternal entombment but, as *Death's Door* shows us, resurrection. Two designs showing the state of the soul after death bring in another of Blake's ideas: after Jesus rends the 'Infernal Veil' and abolishes the 'Druid Law', 'Embraces are Cominglings from the Head even to the Feet'.[3] Hence the erotic embraces in *The meeting of a Family in Heaven* and *The Re-union of the Soul & the Body*.

In general, the published *Grave* designs are more optimistic than Blair's poem would lead one to expect. In illustrating Young, Blake had emphasized the dark and fallen aspects of his subject-matter, but in 1806 he seems to have gone out of his way to find optimistic motifs, emphasizing the theme of regeneration in a Graveyard poem. Of the twelve published designs, only one, *Death of the Strong Wicked Man*, contains no redemptive elements, and this is necessarily so: both in order to make its moral statement and to contrast with the beatific *Death of The Good Old Man*. The two scenes in the recesses of the grave would be pessimistic if they were not preceded by *Christ descending into the Grave* and followed by *Death's Door* and *The Re-union of the Soul & the Body*. Taken in this context, the grave is but a way-station to Eternity,* as we see also in Blake's dedicatory verses 'To the Queen', with their graceful attendant

drawing. Queen Charlotte is addressed as a Thel-like figure, 'Shepherdess of England's Fold', while Blake's persona is a fairy-like winged figure who gives the Queen a true vision of life and death, one from which she will not shrink as Thel had done. 'The Grave is Heaven's golden Gate'—the gate through which the soul, wrapped like a chrysalis, must pass. When the soul awakes from sleep, she 'wond'ring, sees/ In her mild Hand the golden Keys';[4] and in the design which Cromek would not let Blake engrave as a frontispiece, we see her with a key in each hand, floating up towards a Gothic doorway in which there are two distinct keyholes.

The Grave also contains *The Day of Judgment*, a subject Blake was beginning to find compelling in the period around 1806, and which he brought to full fruition with the painting he began after 1809 (see below, pp. 56 and 58, and Notes to the Plates, *Pl.* 50). This engraving (executed by Schiavonetti at a price of sixty guineas, while Blake received only one guinea for the drawing!) is by far the simplest of Blake's Last Judgments. The design stresses a bilateral division between the redeemed on the left and the damned on the right, and it is interesting that the former (with one exception) rise in groups, while the latter fall as individuals. To be damned is to be imprisoned in the self; to be regenerate is to be part of a joyful community. At the lower left are two of the most sensuous of Blake's lovers.

Shortly after the *Grave* débâcle, Blake painted *Sir Jeffrey Chaucer and the nine and twenty Pilgrims on their journey to Canterbury*, a magnificent frieze-like composition (*Pl.* 67), in which just before dawn the Canterbury Pilgrims ride through the arch of the Tabard Inn, its Gothic masonry wonderfully rendered in brownish-grey. The dawn is roseate, beaming with yellow-to-white radiance at the far right; one star is still visible. The central point in the composition is occupied by the cruciform Host, while a pensive Chaucer, evidently

---

* Of course this is the *doctrinal* content of Blair's poem, but the emphasis of the published pictures is far more positive than that of the text. If we also count the six or seven indentifiable rejected designs, the contrast is a bit less marked. These include the 'gothic' *Churchyard Spectres Frightening a Schoolboy* and *The Gambols of the Ghosts According to Their Affections*, as well as the dramatic *Death*

pursuing the Soul Through the Avenues of Life; still, they also include an alternative title-page showing the resurrection of the dead and a wash drawing related to a *Notebook* sketch showing a soul at heaven's gate. 'A widow embracing the turf which covers her husband's grave' is perhaps the most conventionally pathetic piece of all.

modelled after copies of the portrait in Hoccleve's *De Regimine Principum*,[5] brings up the rear. In his *Descriptive Catalogue*, Blake identifies these figures as temporal variations of eternal archetypes. 'Some of the names or titles are altered by time, but the characters themselves for ever remain unaltered, and consequently they are the physiognomies or lineaments of universal human life, beyond which Nature never steps.'[6] And so Blake paints the Wife of Bath as the Whore of Babylon. Her contrary is the Prioress, whose elegance is characteristic of 'the beauty of our ancestors', but an accident in wording has obscured Blake's full meaning here. 'The characters of Women Chaucer has divided into two classes, the Lady Prioress and the Wife of Bath . . . in whose character Chaucer has been equally minute and exact, because she is also a scourge and a blight'.[7] 'Also' here has the force of an intensive; the intention is not to link the Wife with the Prioress and so to make all women forces of evil (*Jerusalem*, after all, is a woman), which would make nonsense of the contrast Blake is stating.

The Chaucer painting was the occasion for a further betrayal of Blake on the part of Robert Hartley Cromek. Cromek evidently saw the picture in Blake's studio, and his remarks led Blake to expect an engraving commission. Cromek, however, went to Thomas Stothard and contracted with him for a new design on the same subject. Blake believed that Stothard was a party to the theft of his idea, but though there can be no question that Stothard's *The Pilgrimage to Canterbury* must have been inspired by an account of Blake's original, it is doubtful that Cromek would have told Stothard where the idea came from. Distrust had long been present between Blake and Stothard (in 1803 Blake says 'H.[ayley] is jealous as Stothard was'[8]), and each was willing to believe the worst of the other. Blake delivered a scathing attack on Stothard in the *Descriptive Catalogue* and wrote vitriolic verses about Stothard, Hayley, and Cromek in his *Notebook*; Stothard twice refused Blake's efforts at reconciliation.[9] Meanwhile, Blake decided to publish his own engraving. In May 1809, he issued a Prospectus, advertising the prospective engraving *Chaucers Canterbury Pilgrims* at a price of four guineas. Something of the nature of Blake's views about art at that time is indicated by the first sentence: 'The Designer proposes to Engrave, in a correct and finished Line manner of Engraving, similar to those original Copper Plates of ALBERT DURER, LUCAS, HISBEN [Hans Sebald Beham], ALDEGRAVE and the old original Engravers . . .'[10] There is something of a manifesto about this beginning, as there is about the engraving itself (*Pl. 68*). In it, Blake returns to the style he had originally learned from Basire, but enriches it with the fruits of his study of early engravings. 'In this Plate', he writes, 'Mr. B. has resumed the style with which he set out in life . . . it is the style of Alb. Durer's Histories & the old Engravers, which cannot be imitated by any one who does not understand drawing . . .'[11] Thus both the painting of Chaucer's Pilgrims and the engraving made after it are intimately related to the ideas about art to which Blake was giving expression at this time.

6. I Have Recollected All My Scattered Thoughts on Art

WE TEND TO THINK OF BLAKE as a vigorous polemicist on subjects relating to the arts, and this is true, but the period of his principal writings about art is limited to little more than a decade, beginning with the letter to Dr Trusler in 1799 and also comprising passages in other letters, the annotations to Reynolds's *Discourses*, the *Descriptive Catalogue* of 1809, and the unfinished *Notebook* manuscript known as the 'Public Address', written about 1810. We may take as an interesting point of perspective the letter Blake addressed to William Hayley on 23 October 1804. 'Suddenly', says Blake, 'on the day after visiting the Truchsessian Gallery of Pictures, I was again enlightened with the light I enjoyed in my youth, and which has for exactly twenty years been closed from me as by a door and by window-shutters . . . I am really drunk with intellectual vision whenever I take a pencil or graver into my hand, even as I used to be in my youth, and as I have not been for twenty dark, but very profitable years.'[1] What was the nature of Blake's experience at the Truchsessian Gallery, and what were its implications for his art?

The collection of Joseph, Count Truchsess, consisting of over 900 paintings, had been brought to London from Vienna in 1803 and was displayed until 1806. Although Truchsess made great claims for his paintings, it appears that Sir Thomas Lawrence was correct in saying that 'There was scarcely an original picture of a *great master* among them' (*The Farington Diary*, 21 August 1803). Nevertheless, the gallery was not a shoddy fraud; rather, like a number of such private collections, it seems to have consisted largely of good copies, many of them studio work. Blake, whose opportunities for seeing paintings were limited, had seldom seen so great a number in one place. Thus comparisons which had preoccupied him for the past two or three years could now be made visually. 'Rembrandt' could be compared to 'Dürer', 'Rubens' to 'Poussin', 'Michelangelo' to 'Salvator Rosa'. After reflecting on the experience for a day, Blake suddenly concluded that the ideas about art which had been evolving in his mind formed a coherent whole. As he was to put it in the *Descriptive Catalogue* (1809), 'Till we get rid of Titian and Correggio, Rubens and Rembrandt, We never shall equal Rafael and Albert Durer, Michael Angelo, and Julio Romano'.[2] To see these ideas in the process of formation, we must briefly consider Blake's annotations to the *Discourses* of Sir Joshua Reynolds.

Some time between 1798 and 1802, Blake acquired a copy of the second edition of the writings of Reynolds, edited in three volumes by Edmund Malone, Reynolds's friend and literary executor. Blake's annotations were written over a period of several years, until at least 1805, during which time he added, deleted, and reinforced comments on Malone's long introduction and on the first eight *Discourses*. On the title-page he set down the burden of his remarks: 'This Man was Hired to Depress Art. This is the Opinion of Will Blake: my Proofs of this Opinion are given in the following Notes.' Although this sounds very much as if Blake's views were diametrically opposed to Reynolds's, it would be more correct to say that they were at an oblique angle to each other—Blake rarely criticized those whose ideas had nothing in common with his own. Someone giving Blake's annotations a cursory reading might easily conclude that Sir Joshua really did prefer Rubens, Rembrandt, and Titian to Raphael and Michelangelo, that he elevated colour above form, that he considered portrait painting the highest type of art, and that he was sympathetic to 'low' subjects showing boors drinking. Actually, almost the opposite is true. Like Blake, Reynolds thought that history painting was the highest art, though the two artists defined it differently. Reynolds, too, considered Raphael and Michelangelo the supreme artists and relegated the Venetian and Flemish schools to a much lower status. Both admired Poussin; they really did disagree about Titian and Dürer. But the central point at issue was not the assessment of individual artists.

According to the traditional hierarchy of modes, which Reynolds endorsed, history painting was the highest form of art, corresponding to the literary epic.

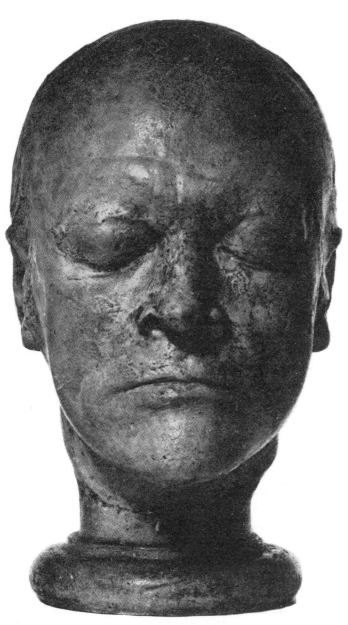

FIG. 7 J. S. DEVILLE: *Life Mask of William Blake*. About 1807. Plaster. 11½ in. high. Cambridge, Fitzwilliam Museum

Landscape and portraiture were lower modes, but each possessed its own inner laws, and even the lowest modes —like ornamental flower painting—were deserving of attention. One could by a certain measure of idealization raise a middle mode like landscape or portraiture higher; hence the peculiar position of Claude's

imaginary landscapes and, one suspects, of Reynolds's portraits. But there could be no mixed modes, for 'Nothing has its proper lustre but in its proper place' (*Discourse* V). Claude erred in introducing mythological figures into his landscapes, as did Richard Wilson. Similar to the hierarchy of modes was the hierarchy of cultures. The Roman, Florentine, and Bolognese schools 'are the great schools of the world in this epick style'. The greatest French artists such as Poussin were 'a colony from the Roman school'. Below these came the Venetian, Flemish, and Dutch, 'all professing to depart from the great purposes of painting and catching at applause by inferior qualities'.

There is much that Blake could agree with here, and sometimes his annotations do express grudging approval. But for Blake only the topmost mode exists. The Florentine and Roman schools *are* art; the rest is consigned to outer darkness. Illusionism, theatrical tricks, richness of colour—all these are manners of seducing the mind from Form. The intellectual content of the work of art as perceived through its forms is the only value. Therefore a small picture by Blake is likely to be as pregnant with meaning as a large one. Everything the artist lays his hand to is part of an overall grand design: to elucidate the meaning of reality. 'The Greek Gems are in the Same Style as the Greek Statues.'[3]

Furthermore, these attitudes towards art (and concomitantly towards the education of artists) are based upon models of the mind. Reynolds's is derived from the school of Locke, Blake's from the school of Plato. At the head of *Discourse* VIII Blake writes:

Burke's Treatise on the Sublime & Beautiful is founded on the Opinions of Newton & Locke; on this Treatise Reynolds has grounded many of his assertions in all his Discourses. I read Burke's Treatise when very Young; at the same time I read Locke on Human Understanding & Bacon's Advancement of Learning; on Every one of these Books I wrote my Opinions, & on looking them over find that my Notes on Reynolds in this Book are exactly Similar. I felt the Same Contempt & Abhorrence then that I do now. They mock Inspiration & Vision.[4]

For Reynolds nothing is in the mind that was not first in the senses; memory stores our sensory data, imagination recombines them. Although this can result in a mechanical plan of the mind, it must be said that, as he goes on, Sir Joshua gives more and more weight to the imagination, warning in *Discourse* XIII against 'an unfounded distrust of the imagination and feeling'. And so the Gothic, so dear to Blake's own imagination, is elevated above even the classical in *Discourse* XIII: 'Gothick architecture; which, though not so ancient as the Grecian, is more so to our imagination, with which the artist is more concerned than with absolute truth.' Here we do see the limits of Reynolds's idea of imagination, even at its highest, from Blake's point of view—it is still a maker of fictions. For Blake the imagination is cognitive. In operation it is 'Con- or Innate Science'.[5] Inspiration is not, as Reynolds would have it, a metaphor: 'The Ancients did not mean to Impose when they affirm'd their belief in Vision & Revelation. Plato was in Earnest: Milton was in Earnest. They believ'd that God did visit Man Really & Truly & not as Reynolds pretends.'[6]

And so when Reynolds speaks of central form, he means something quite different from Blake's Forms. Central form is abstracted by the imagination from the memories of accumulated sensory experience; Blake's Forms are 'Perfect in the Poet's mind, but these are not Abstracted nor Compounded from Nature, but are from Imagination'.[7] Blake accuses Reynolds of believing that Genius may be taught. Actually, Sir Joshua believes no such thing, but he does believe that imagination can be cultivated. Had he had an opportunity to annotate Blake, he would probably have replied in the vein of the so-called 'Ironical Discourse', unpublished in his lifetime, in which he satirized Barry:

It is with great regret that I see so many students labouring day after day in the Academy, as if they imagined that a liberal art, as ours is, was to be acquired like a mechanical trade, by dint of labour, or I may add the absurdity of supposing that it could be acquired by any means whatever. We know that if you are born with a genius, labour is unnecessary; if you have it not, labour is in vain; genius is all in all.[8]

But of course it was not to labour that Blake objected; the question at issue is that of the truth of the imagination. For Blake, this truth is inseparable from all aspects of life—personal, political, philosophical, artistic. In the annotations Blake is in effect painting the Spiritual Form of a man whose idea of the mind is that of a *camera obscura*. Thus isolated in what Norman O. Brown has termed 'Universal Otherhood', he embraces an eclectic idea of art which, while seeming to honour Raphael and Michelangelo, actually leads students to succumb to the delusive goddess Nature, as manifested by the seductive Titian. Having abandoned the Eternal Forms of his own Imagination, he founds a corrupt institution, fawning on royal patronage; he paints society portraits which William Hazlitt was to describe as 'half made-up and faded beauties . . . which comparatively resembled paste figures smeared over with paint'.[9] And he incurs the prophetic wrath of William Blake, howling in the wilderness.

Blake's attitude towards art in general and towards Reynolds in particular had not always been thus uncompromising. As late as 1799, we find him trying to balance out the different schools. 'If you approve of my Manner', he writes to Dr Trusler, '& it is agreeable to you, I would rather Paint Pictures in oil of the same dimensions than make Drawings, & on the same terms; by this means you will have a number of Cabinet pictures, which I flatter myself will not be unworthy of a Scholar of Rembrandt & Teniers, whom I have Studied no less than Rafael & Michael angelo.'[10] Even in 1802, he quotes with approval from Reynolds's published letter to William Gilpin, in which Reynolds assigns the picturesque a low place in the hierarchy of modes. 'So Says Sir Joshua', writes Blake to Thomas Butts, 'and So say I', going on to allow a place for various kinds of artists. 'Carrache's Pictures are not like Correggio's, nor Correggio's like Rafael's; &, if neither of them was to be encouraged till he did like any of the others, he must die without Encouragement.'[11] But here Blake is clearly interested only in the upper part of the hierarchy of modes, in Raphael not in Correggio.

This is a transitional phase which ends with the utter condemnation of Flemish and Venetian painting in general and particularly of Rubens, Titian, and

Correggio, whose past influence he acknowledges in the *Descriptive Catalogue* of 1809, though he now vehemently rejects it.

> The spirit of Titian was particularly active in raising doubts concerning the possibility of executing without a model, and when once he had raised the doubt, it became easy for him to snatch away the vision time after time, for, when the Artist took his pencil to execute his ideas, his power of imagination weakened so much and darkened, that memory of nature, and of Pictures of the various schools possessed his mind, instead of appropriate execution resulting from the inventions; like walking in another man's style, or speaking, or looking in another man's style and manner, unappropriate and repugnant to your own individual character; tormenting the true Artist, till he leaves the Florentine, and adopts the Venetian practice, or does as Mr. B. has done, has the courage to suffer poverty and disgrace, till he ultimately conquers.
>
> Rubens is a most outrageous demon, and by infusing the remembrances of his Pictures and style of execution, hinders all power of individual thought: so that the man who is possessed by this demon loses all admiration of any other Artist but Rubens and those who were his imitators and journeymen; he causes to the Florentine and Roman Artist fear to execute; and though the original conception was all fire and animation, he loads it with hellish brownness, and blocks up all its gates of light except one, and that one he closes with iron bars, till the victim is obliged to give up the Florentine and Roman practice, and adopt the Venetian and Flemish.
>
> Correggio is a soft and effeminate, and consequently a most cruel demon, whose whole delight is to cause endless labour to whoever suffers him to enter his mind.[12]

Blake even exhibited three pictures displaying the influence of these 'demons', classifying them in the *Descriptive Catalogue* as 'Experiment Pictures' (nos. VII and VIII are untraced but IX—*Satan calling up his Legions* [*Pl. 65*]—is in the Victoria and Albert Museum). Ironically, Blake is here in agreement with Reynolds (who, however, made allowance for Titian). Reynolds warns his students in *Discourse* IV that Veronese and Tintoretto

> are the persons who may be said to have exhausted all the powers of florid eloquence, to debauch the young and inexperienced, and have without doubt, been the cause of turning off the attention of the connoisseur and patron of art, as well as that of the painter, from those higher excellencies of which the art is capable, and which ought to be required in every considerable production. By them, and their imitators, a style merely ornamental has been disseminated through all Europe. Rubens carried it to Flanders . . .

Clearly, Blake had an eclectic middle period, during which he was willing to absorb lessons in colourism and chiaroscuro from sources which he later rejected as inimical to true art. We will see the results in discussing his illustrations to the Bible. The visit to the Truchsessian Gallery was not an initiatory but a confirmatory experience, bringing to intense critical awareness doubts which he had experienced for several years previously. In his writings about art—the annotations to Reynolds, the *Descriptive Catalogue*, and the so-called 'Public Address'—he dogmatically asserted the position he had reached, and in his paintings and drawings of this period he gave expression to these principles. To build up a painting out of masses of colour was to yield to the seduction of the phenomenal world: the true end of art was Form rendered through hard, determinate outline. One need not sympathize with Blake's view of Rembrandt, Titian and Rubens to realize that this exclusionary process was necessary to his development as an artist, just as one need not reject Milton in order to understand what Keats meant in saying 'Life to him would be death to me.'

Blake's method in his polemical writings is reiterative, and he tends to repeat his fundamental principles, together with his examples of Roman and Florentine grandeur versus the 'Venetian and Flemish ooze & slime'. There are, however, two further ideas in his prose after 1800 (and in passages of *Milton* and *Jerusalem* as well) that should be mentioned here. One concerns the archetypal nature of art, already touched on in relation to the *Canterbury Pilgrims*; the other involves Blake's new attitude towards the political economy of art.

Blake's view of the origin of the artist's image is that it is a reification of an archetype that, unlike Reynolds's central form, really exists. In *Jerusalem*[13] the realm of these essences is Los's Halls, which are filled with 'bright Sculptures' in which 'All things acted on Earth are seen'. The *Descriptive Catalogue* gives a similar but more personal account of the origins of the spiritual portraits of Pitt and Nelson, described as

> compositions of a mythological cast, similar to those Apotheoses of Persian, Hindoo, and Egyptian Antiquity, which are still preserved on rude monuments, being copies from some stupendous originals now lost or perhaps buried till some happier age. The Artist having been taken in vision into the ancient republics, monarchies, and patriarchates of Asia, has seen those wonderful originals called in the Sacred Scriptures the Cherubim, which were sculptured and painted on walls of Temples, Towers, Cities, Palaces, and erected . . . among the Rivers of Paradise, being originals from which the Greeks and Hetrurians copied Hercules Farnese, Venus of Medicis, Apollo Belvidere, and all the grand works of ancient art.[14]

This passage brings in another favourite idea of the later Blake: the great Greek exemplars of Neoclassical art were not, after all, the highest forms of human expression, but were merely pallid imitations of more ancient Eastern works. Whether these works seen in vision were identical to the archetypes themselves, the actual 'bright Sculptures of Los's Halls', or simply closer to the archetypes than the supposed derivations of Greece and Italy, is not clear. The idea that such 'stupendous originals' had existed was not peculiar to Blake, although he does give it an anti-classical bias not necessarily found elsewhere. James Barry had lectured on the 'colossal statues' of the Assyrians, on the bas-reliefs of animals raised on the walls around the palace of Semiramis, and on the 'historical representations, which were vitrified, or enamelled, on the brick walls of Babylon . . .' Barry goes on to speak of the cherubim as works of art 'sculptured on the mercy-seat'

and points out that 'the Assyrians, Egyptians, Phenicians, Persians, and the other oriental nations, had cultivated the arts long before the Greeks . . .' To Barry all these facts suggest an antediluvian origin: 'It will be difficult to reconcile this aggregate of things with the duration and circumstances of any known people existing in that period of time between Abraham and Noah. To me these broken, unconnected knowledges seem to carry evident marks of being really the wrecks and vestiges which might have been preserved after such a general catastrophe as the Deluge . . .'[15] Blake uses this notion of the unoriginality of Greek art to support his post-1800 view that even the greatest of artists and poets were 'curb'd by the general malady & infection from the silly Greek & Latin slaves of the Sword' (*Milton*).[16] No longer is his purpose 'to renew the lost Art of the Greeks', as he had expressed it to Dr Trusler as late as 1799.[17]

Blake's view of the relation between art and commerce had changed similarly. In *America*, the citizens are pictured closing their books and locking their chests in fear of the plagues of Albion's Angel, and 'The mariners of Boston drop their anchors and unlade';[18] these peaceable burghers become the 'fierce Americans' who triumph over their oppressors. Blake himself had pursued trade with sanguine optimism from the time of his short-lived partnership with James Parker in 1784. In 1800 we find him praising the higher order of commerce he now finds in London: 'I. . . find that in future to live will not be so difficult as it has been. It is very Extraordinary that London in so few years from a City of meer Necessaries or at l[e]ast a commerce of the lowest order of luxuries should have become a City of Elegance in some degree & that its once stupid inhabitants should enter into an Emulation of Grecian manners.' (Letter to George Cumberland.)[19] Bitter experience with Cromek and the disappointment of his dearest expectations had convinced Blake that the spirit of commerce was inimical to art. 'Commerce is so far from being beneficial to Arts, or to Empires, that it is destructive of both . . .'[20] There is personal bitterness here, but there is also a sense of the organic relationship between art and society. A debased society can value only a debased art. Blake sees 'the wretched State of the Arts in this Country & in Europe' as 'originating in the wretched State of Political Science'.[21] Once more in this he follows Barry, who ended his first lecture with an attack on government payments to newspapers and began the second with the proposition that tyranny is destructive of art. 'Nothing', says Barry, 'can be a greater bar and impediment to the advancement and dignified exertion of art, than a mean, grovelling, and contracted disposition in the artist.'

Blake brings these various strands together in his *Laocoön* engraving (*Pl.* 95), which, though executed about 1818, may appropriately be discussed at this point. The engraving was a by-product of a purely commercial job: he had been commissioned to do plates illustrating Flaxman's essay about sculpture for Rees's *Cyclopaedia*, and for this purpose he made a drawing of the Royal Academy's cast of the Laocoön group. ('Why Mr Blake', said Fuseli, 'you a student[!] you might teach us.')[22] This task gave Blake the idea for a separate plate, in which he surrounded the figures with aphoristic statements about art. These represent Blake's views at their most uncompromising. 'Where any view of Money exists Art cannot be carried on, but War only'; 'Christianity is Art & not Money/Money is its Curse'; 'Art Degraded Imagination Denied War Governed the Nations'. To the piece as a whole Blake gave the title 'ה' & his two Sons Satan & Adam as they were copied from the Cherubim of Solomons Temple by three Rhodians & applied to Natural Fact or History of Ilium.' This, then, is based on one of those stupendous originals. The Greeks who copied it thought they were depicting a priest and his sons being crushed by two serpents before the walls of Troy, but actually the original vision concerned Jehovah, the father of both the natural man and the separated will, all struggling together in the toils of the material world. Thus the *Laocoön* engraving consummates the themes which had preoccupied Blake in his writings about art a decade or so earlier: the archetypal nature of art, the priority of Hebrew over Classical renditions of the archetypes, and the incompatibility of true art with the commercial spirit.

7. The Sublime of the Bible

IN 1799 BLAKE received an order from his friend Thomas Butts[1] for 'Fifty small pictures at One Guinea each'.[2] These were temperas on Biblical subjects and were but the first group of a much larger number of illustrations to the Bible that Blake was to execute for Butts. Taken together, 212 individual pictures executed by Blake in the course of his career are classified as Bible illustrations; of these the astonishing number of 155 are known to have been purchased by Thomas Butts. This number is all the more remarkable when we consider that at least some of the Bible illustrations not owned by Butts must have been completed before the friendship began (the *Joseph* series, for example, and *The Sacrifice of Isaac*). It is clear that, had it not been for an obscure civil servant, the vast majority of Blake's Bible pictures might well have remained unpainted, for Blake would almost certainly have been forced into spending even more time engraving for the publishers were it not for the small but steady income he received from Butts. The pictures are of course now widely dispersed and some are untraced, but it is possible to reconstruct the evolution of Blake's Biblical art and also to discuss the manner in which Blake interpreted the Bible through these paintings and drawings.

The Butts series of fifty temperas (1799–1800) is remarkable for the diversity of influences that may be discerned there. As Bindman remarks, the use of light in *The Nativity* owes something to Rembrandt, while there is a Titianesque quality to *Bathsheba at the Bath* with its warm, sensuous colours.[3] Another richly coloured painting, *Lot and His Daughters*, may owe something to Rubens. The rose-coloured background behind Christ's blue nimbus in *Christ's Entry into Jerusalem* (Pl. 79) has a Venetian effect, and, despite sad deterioration, it is evident that *The Agony in the Garden* was once intensely coloured, as is the restored *Christ Blessing Little Children*. Having made this point, we must also be aware that Blake did not pursue only strange gods in the tempera series. *The Last Supper* (Pl. 80), for example, is based compositionally on a painting by Poussin— *The Eucharist* of *The Seven Sacraments*, exhibited in Lon-

don as part of the Orleans Collection in 1798, and Blake's admiration for Poussin was not to diminish. Also, Blake's own mark is unmistakable in *The Nativity*, as the infant Jesus leaps in a nimbus of light from the swooning Mary towards the arms of Elizabeth. Nor must it be thought that because of its special, experimental nature the tempera series is without iconographical meaning. In *The Circumcision* (Pl. 76), for example, Blake presents an event that he was to develop symbolically in *Jerusalem*, where he speaks of 'Circumcising the excrementitious/Husk & Covering',[4] following the Old Testament meaning of circumcision as a ritual of purification. In *The Baptism of Christ* (Pl. 75), none of the earthly spectators look directly at Christ's divine humanity; instead their gaze is directed either down into the water or up towards the celestial beings in the sky. In general, however, the tempera series probably emphasizes 'painterly' values more than it does symbolism and displays a willingness, unusual for Blake, to assimilate a variety of styles. He was shortly to conclude that he had been mistaken in this and that he had to return to the primitive origins of his art. (The tempera *Entombment*, with its statuesque symmetry, shows the direction in which Blake's art would move a few years later.) This evidently caused Butts some confusion and even offence, for we find Blake writing to him on 22 November 1802: 'I have now proved that the parts of the art which I had neglected to display in those little pictures & drawings which I had the pleasure & profit to do for you, are incompatible with the designs'.[5]

Evidently the difficulty with Butts was smoothed over, for on 6 July 1803 Blake sent Butts a *Riposo* and announced 'I now have on the Stocks the following drawings for you: 1. Jephthah sacrificing his Daughter; 2. Ruth & her mother in Law & Sister; 3. The three Maries at the Sepulcher; 4. The Death of Joseph; 5. The Death of the Virgin Mary; 6. St Paul Preaching; & 7. The Angel of the Divine Presence clothing Adam & Eve with Coats of Skins.'[6] In these watercolours Blake abandons the experiments with chiaroscuro and colourism attempted in the tempera series. At the same time there is a growth of particularly Blakean meaning. *Jephthah sacrificing his Daughter* shows the sacrifice of an emanation, similar to Urizen's casting-off of Ahania. There is something decidedly unsettling about the Angel of the Divine Presence: figures of superhuman stature are seldom up to any good in Blake, and the clothing covers the nakedness which is the work of God. The three bewildered Marys seem to close together defensively against the angel's message that Christ is risen.

In the watercolours that Blake did for Butts about 1805 the tendency towards strong linearity and hard outline increases even further, as can be seen in *The Angels hovering over the Body of Jesus in the Sepulchre* (*Pl.* 84), later exhibited at the Royal Academy in 1808 and in Blake's own exhibition of 1809. The symmetry of the composition, the beautiful Gothic arch formed by the wings of the Angels, and the subdued role of colour all differentiate this picture sharply from the temperas of 1799–1800. As Butlin says, 'Those [watercolours] of 1805 show a considerable move away from the forceful-ness of the 1790s, reverting, though now in a completely personal way, to the neo-classicism of Blake's early works. They are characterized by clarity of composition, of outline, and of distinct fields of colour.'[7] This development is a manifestation of the programme Blake had embarked on after the Truchsessian Gallery experience, and these pictures are distinctly related to his writings about art, already discussed. Blake's own views seem to enter all the more, as in the depictions of Moses, whose role as a transmitter of Law is conveyed by his diminutive, abject figure in *God Writing Upon the Tables of the Covenant* (*Pl.* 32). In Numbers, Moses saved the people by erecting a brass serpent on a pole to heal the bites of the fiery serpents, but in *Moses Erecting the Brazen Serpent* (*Pl.* 73), Moses himself is wrapped around by the serpent of materialism as he gazes at the idol he has erected. The symbolism of *Christ in the Carpenter's Shop* is also interesting. Here Blake has Christ holding an enormous pair of com-passes in his right hand, showing that even this instru-ment of Reason can be integrated with spiritual vision —no object in Blake's symbolism is ever completely positive or negative except as defined by context. Of

course some of the 1805 watercolours make their effect felt through their visual aspect alone. In *Mary Magdalen at the Sepulchre* (*Pl.* 83) we see a spiritual counterpart, as it were, to Rembrandt's chiaroscuro: the radiance suffusing the face and upper body of Christ, the face of Mary Magdalen and the two angels cannot come from a single external light source but must be inner and spiritual. The simple device of having all save Christ turn away from the *Woman Taken in Adultery* (*Pl.* 81) creates a startling effect, one which is enriched if we recognize in Christ's writing finger the New Dispen-sation's counterpart to the finger of God writing on the Tables of the Covenant. The Old Testament God has his back to us; Jesus bows in a graceful arc before the accused adulteress. Still other pictures draw upon tradition rather than being Blake's own creation. This is especially true of such illustrations to Revelation as *The Four and Twenty Elders Casting Their Crowns Before the Divine Throne* (*Pl.* 82) and *The Great Red Dragon and the Woman Clothed with the Sun* (*Pl.* 85). Yet even such pictures are seldom without some special dimension of meaning. In *The Four and Twenty Elders* the four visages glimpsed behind the dark throne are indeed the emblems of the four Evangelists, but they are also Blake's Four Zoas.

Some of the late Bible illustrations painted in tempera in 1810 are even more anti-naturalistic than the 1805 watercolours. *Adam naming the Beasts* (*Pl.* 77), *Eve naming the Birds*, and *The Virgin and Child in Egypt* (*Pl.* 78) all have a primitive, hieratic quality reminiscent of early Italian painting. Blake did no further Bible illustrations for Butts after 1810, but in 1811 or later Butts pur-chased *An Allegory of the Spiritual Condition of Man*, Blake's largest surviving painting, which has border illustrations depicting the cycle of sacred history from Creation to Last Judgment.

The Last Judgment itself is the subject of a Butts watercolour dated 1806, followed by a pendant, *The Fall of Man* (*Pl.* 49), in 1807. This *Last Judgment* is considerably more complex and detailed than the one Blake had drawn for Blair's *Grave*, also in 1806, and it was followed by two even more elaborate ones, a water-colour for the wife of Lord Egremont (*Pl.* 50) in 1808 and a pen and wash drawing over pencil purchased by

FIG. 8 *Mrs Blake*. After 1802. Pencil. 11¼ × 8¾ in. Drawn on the back of a proof sheet of Hayley's *Ballads*. London, Tate Gallery

Butts about 1810. All these were related to the now lost tempera painting heightened with gold, *A Vision of the Last Judgment*, which Blake describes and interprets in his *Notebook*.[8] The main compositional differences among the three surviving *Last Judgments* are that in the 1806 Butts picture Blake placed the Whore of Babylon in the bottom centre with the seven-headed dragon above her, while in the two later drawings he reversed these positions, creating a kind of grotto for the dragon and seating the Whore on top of it; also in 1806, and again in 1810, three angelic trumpeters swoop downwards in the centre, but in 1808 there are four winged angelic trumpeters standing upright. Of course there are many differences of detail which can only be understood by a close examination of the works themselves. Fortunately, Blake wrote out an explanation of the 1808 drawing for his friend the painter Ozias Humphrey, who was going blind.[9] He also wrote a short scenario on the back of the pendant, *The Fall of Man*.[10] Taken together, these two subjects frame all of human history in the fallen world, and it is only fitting that Thomas Butts should have owned versions of each.

8. Milton Lov'd Me in Childhood
& Shew'd Me His Face

THROUGHOUT HIS CREATIVE LIFE, Blake waged a lover's quarrel with John Milton, with whom he wrestled as his own Milton did with Urizen, trying to flesh the Spectrous part of Milton's identity with the red clay of life. His first attack comes in *The Marriage of Heaven and Hell*: 'Note: The reason Milton wrote in fetters when he wrote of Angels & God, and at liberty when of Devils & Hell, is because he was a true Poet and of the Devil's party without knowing it.'[1] In this ironical passage, frequently misunderstood, Blake is not saying that Satan is heroic. Rather, his argument is that Milton invested Satan with energies that properly belong to Jesus, leaving 'the Son a Ratio of the five senses, & the Holy-ghost Vacuum!' Blake would surely have agreed with Shelley that Milton's Satan is marked by 'the traits of ambition, envy, revenge, and a desire for personal aggrandisement'.[2] Blake's point is that Milton projected his own libidinal energies, which he feared, into a figure named Satan; while whatever these energies may be called, they characterize the true Messiah. His ambivalence towards Milton continued into the nineteenth century. In *Milton a Poem* he enlarges on the view that 'Milton's Religion is the cause: there is no end to destruction'.[3] Yet in 1804, the date on the *Milton* title-page, he could also write 'I have the happiness of seeing the Divine countenance in such men as Cowper and Milton more distinctly than in any prince or hero.'[4] In *Milton a Poem* and in interpretative illustrations to Milton's major works, Blake worked out the tension between these two views.

On 25 April 1803, Blake wrote to Thomas Butts: 'I have in these three years composed an immense number of verses on One Grand Theme, Similar to Homer's Iliad or Milton's Paradise Lost, the Persons & Machinery intirely new to the Inhabitants of Earth (some of the Persons Excepted).' As the subject is described as 'the Spiritual Acts of my three years' Slumber on the banks of the Ocean',[5] this long poem must be *Milton*, which includes a *roman à clef* about Blake, Hayley, and some other Persons not entirely new to the inhabitants of Earth. The date 1804 appears on the etched title-

page, but two references to 'Hand' (a symbolic character associated with Blake's exhibition of 1809) in the poem and an allusion made about 1810 to 'a Poem concerning my Three years' Herculean Labours at Felpham, which I will soon Publish',[6] throws the date of issue back to 1810. There are four extant copies. Copy A (British Museum) and Copy B (Huntington Library) each comprise forty-five plates, some of the leaves bearing the watermark 1808. In copy C (New York Public Library), Blake added six plates. Three of these, 3[a], 4[b], 10[c],* expand the allegory of Blake's conflict with Hayley and add a further mythical background to it. Additional plate 18 [d] brings back Orc, for whom Blake had anticipated a role in the poem but not developed it further. Additional plate 32 [e] introduces the distinction between Individuals and States, an important feature of Blake's later thought. In copy D (Lessing J. Rosenwald Collection), Blake added yet another plate, 5 [f], to the Bard's prophetic Song. This copy was produced no earlier than 1815, as indicated by watermarks. Curiously, copies C and D lack the Preface, with its famous lyric beginning 'And did those feet in ancient time'; and so no single original copy of *Milton* is complete.

In addition to these differences in foliation, the four copies display some interesting differences in technique. Copy A was painted in light watercolour over a black-printed base. B was similarly painted and also touched with gold, C likewise. D was painted much more heavily over red printing and touched considerably with gold. This last copy, then, contrasts significantly with the other three. Although it is indeed a magnificent work of art, its glories should not blind us to the somewhat subtler beauties of the other copies. Blake achieved the grand colour-effects of D at a certain cost, frequently painting over the stipple and white line effects on the printed plates. Consequently, copies A, B and C have more the character of works of graphic

---

* In order to retain the sense of sequence of *Milton*, I follow the foliation of the Rosenwald copy, which is also that of *The Illuminated Blake*, instead of that of the *Census*.

art heightened by watercolour, D the character of a series of watercolours over an etched base. The stylistic differences have thematic implications as well. For example, the flesh colours in D are reassuringly warm and sensuous, unlike the strange rosy and purplish flesh tones of A, B and C, where Blake seems to be deliberately striving for the effect of a primitive icon. In the first three copies, the ground beneath Milton's feet and the contoured backgrounds are almost always green, suggesting 'England's green & pleasant Land', while this is frequently not the case in D. Of course we would not like to do without either alternative; but we should bear in mind that both alternatives exist.

Milton was the longest and most ambitious illuminated book produced by Blake so far, yet its designs appear to show a retrogression from the complex composite art form of *America* to his earlier, more illustrative conception of the interrelation of text and design. However, the *Milton* designs are subtle and at times ambiguous; what appears to be mere illustration often turns out to be symbolic statement. There are ten full-page plates (some of them bearing inscriptions or a line of text), and numerous minor designs, marginal and interlinear, of half a page or less. Our consideration here must necessarily be limited to the major designs.

In *Milton*, plate 1 (*Pl.* 53), we see Milton about to descend into the Vortex of material nature. His profile bears some resemblance to the head of Milton (*Pl.* 69) Blake had done for Hayley's library after some engraved version of the Faithorne portrait, but this is Milton's spiritual form, 'Unhappy tho' in heav'n'.[7] Having descended to the world of Generation, Milton divests himself of 'the robe of the promise', that garment which is the excrementitious husk of the literal cloaking the spiritual, and stands in plate 16 [*Census* 13] as an exemplar of the human form divine (*Pl.* 54). His strangely dark body in copies A and B and his white nimbus give him the effect of a primitive Christ. Next he must wrestle with Urizen in plate 18 [*Census* 15] 'To Annihilate the Self-hood of Deceit & False Forgiveness' (*Pl.* 52).[8] Urizen is once more a Jehovah-figure whose hands rest on the Tables of the Law; they strive on the banks of the Arnon—the river that runs into the Dead Sea—but unlike Urizen, Milton does not go into the water. On the hill above them a youth and maidens, illuminated by the sun's radiance, disport with musical instruments. This battle goes on all through the poem, the one giving death and the other giving life, until on plate 45 [*Census* 41] Urizen collapses like a rag doll in Milton's arms. In all four of these full-page illustrations, though less so in copy D than in the others, there is a stark, non-naturalistic effect, heightened by the use of white line engraving.

William Blake himself appears in two other full-page designs and his brother Robert in one. Plate 47 [*Census* 21] shows the crouching Blake looking back to see Los in the sun, an experience Blake had written of in verses sent in a letter to Thomas Butts on 22 November 1802 as well as in *Milton*, plate 22:[9]

> And Los behind me stood, a terrible flaming Sun, just close
> Behind my back. I turned round in terror, and behold!
> Los stood in that fierce glowing fire . . .

Blake originally placed the full-page design after the related text, but shifted it back towards the end of the poem in copies C and D, both for dramatic emphasis and in order to further indicate the timeless nature of the event. On Blake's right foot in the picture he wears one of the sandals 'I bound . . . On to walk forward thro' Eternity'. Again, as if to bring out the concurrency of all events, the visionary experience described on plate 15 is the subject of a full-page design (*Fig.* 9) on plate 32 [*Census* 29]. In this plate, inscribed 'William', Milton as a falling star enters Blake's left foot 'falling on the tarsus', which, as Erdman points out, makes Blake's conversionary experience parallel with that of Saul of Tarsus.[10] Blake falls back in ecstasy, cruciform and palms up, ending the first book of *Milton*. In plate 37 [*Census* 33], inscribed 'Robert' (*Pl.* 55), Blake's dead brother is pictured in the reversed posture of falling back to the right as the star enters his right foot. This symbolism, the right indicating the spiritual and the left the material, prefigures the right-left symbolism of the *Job* series.

The three remaining full-page plates of *Milton* have been variously interpreted. Some see the figure in flames in plate 10 [*Census* 8] as Rintrah, some as Orc, and the identification affects the other two figures. The latter look enough like Los and Enitharmon as they are pictured elsewhere to suggest that the flaming figure on the plinth is Orc, who was to have had a major role in *Milton* before Blake changed his plan for the work. The male and female in post-coital gloom in plate 42 [*Census* 38] with an eagle above them (*Pl.* 56) are described not in *Milton* but in *Jerusalem* as Albion and England:

Over them the famish'd Eagle screams on boney
    Wings, and around
Them howls the Wolf of famine; deep heaves the
    Ocean black ...   94:15–16[11]

FIG. 9 *Milton*, copy A, plate 32 (*Census* 29). 1804–9. Relief etching, painted in watercolour. 6½ × 4½ in. London, British Museum

The ultimate plate, bearing the line 'To go forth to the Great Harvest & Vintage of the Nations', pictures two human ears of corn, between which stands Milton's emanation Ololon.

In *Milton* Blake addresses himself to what he believed to be the errors of the poet most important to him. John Milton had been divinely inspired, but he had rejected his female component, as represented by the amalgamated figure Blake creates of Milton's wives and daughters; and he had—wrongly, in Blake's view—taken an active role in the religious-political warfare of his day, thus joining Calvin and Luther, who 'in fury premature/ Sow'd War and stern division between Papists & Protestants'.[12] Blake incorporates similar strictures in his illustrative interpretations of Milton's poems, though here he could not be as programmatic as he was in his own composite work.

He executed designs for six of Milton's major works, which, with the repetition of three of these subjects, may be tabulated as follows:

1801   *Comus*. Patron: Rev. Joseph Thomas
              Present location: Huntington Art Gallery

c. 1810–15 *Comus*. Patron: Thomas Butts
              Present location: Boston Museum of Fine Arts

c. 1807   *Paradise Lost*. Patron: Rev. Joseph Thomas
               Present location: Huntington Art Gallery

1808   *Paradise Lost*. Patron: Thomas Butts
              Present location: 9 in Boston Museum, 1 in Huntington Art Gallery, 1 in Houghton Library, 1 in Victoria and Albert Museum

1809   *Hymn on the Morning of Christ's Nativity*. Patron: Rev. Joseph Thomas
              Present location: Whitworth Gallery, Manchester

1815–16? *Hymn on the Morning of Christ's Nativity*. Patron: Thomas Butts
              Present location: Huntington Art Gallery

c. 1815–18 *Paradise Regained*. Patron: John Linnell (in 1825)
              Present location: Fitzwilliam Museum

c. 1816   *L'Allegro* and *Il Penseroso*. Patron: Thomas Butts
              Present location: Pierpont Morgan Library

The three series which Blake repeated display, as one would expect, stylistic differences; but his conceptual approach to the poems did not change, and so we may take them in the order in which he first illustrated them.

Comus does not seem an especially auspicious subject for Blake; indeed, in order to render it in his own terms he would have had virtually to invert Milton's meaning, which he appears to have been unwilling to do. His designs stay close to the text, though there are of course signs of his own imagination throughout. The animal-headed shapes which appear in the first design (*Pl.* 64) are in Milton's stage direction, and Blake has purposely made them appear more like masquers than monsters. Comus is naked in the Thomas set, but in the generally richer and more embellished Butts set, he wears a skin-tight costume and holds a glass in one hand as well as his 'charming rod' in the other; and in the later version the Lady's Attendant Spirit has temporarily disappeared. He is present in both examples of no. 2, in the earlier as an angelic figure bearing a golden flower, in the later as a mime figure making a gesture of helplessness. The Lady is in the situation of a Thel tempted by the Voice of Experience, and the flower seems fresh from the Garden of Love (present only in the Thomas version, it is not in Milton's text at this point, but it will be introduced in line 633). Next the brothers are seen as described by Comus, plucking grapes. In the Thomas version, their swords lie together on the ground while Comus still has his phallic wand, and there is a homoerotic suggestion in their rapt interchange of glances. They regain their swords in no. 4 under the tutelage of the Attendant Spirit, 'habited like a Shepherd'. Under his left arm, the Spirit holds the positive counterpart of Comus's wand, a shepherd's crook; in his right hand he holds the flower haemony, which has medicinal powers greater than those of the moly with which Odysseus overcame Circe's enchantment. Overhead, Hecate drives her dragon car, representative of those forces of mere nature which the Spirit is teaching the brothers to overcome. Meanwhile, at the enchanted palace, Comus is busy tempting the Lady with images of the fecundity of nature. The enchanted chair in which she sits is decorated with human figures bound around with serpents in the Thomas version. To the rescue come the brothers, wresting away Comus's cup of intoxication but failing to deprive him of his wand. And so the lady must sit a while longer until disenchanted by Sabrina in no. 7. (Sabrina, the murdered daughter of Locrine, will become one of the Daughters of Albion in *Jerusalem*.) Then Blake seems deliberately to avoid the rich, Beulah-like possibilities of imagery in the Spirit's eulogy, in order to rush on to the restoration of the Lady to her parents in no. 8. This aged couple look too much like Har and Heva for comfort, and indicate something of Blake's disquietude with the whole theme. One could read the series as a projection of two alternatives equally unacceptable to Blake: Comus's duplicitous seductiveness and the Lady's fear of the forces of life, which is suggested in the Thomas series by the folding of her hands across her chest in nos. 5 and 6.

Paradise Lost presented Blake with a subject that he could interpret with much greater conviction, for he too believed in a Fall. Thus the consistency and power in these designs are compatible with a certain freedom of interpretation, Blake undoubtedly believing that he was revealing Milton's true, underlying meaning. The pictures in the second series are larger than those in the first, and, writes Butlin, 'the figures . . . are marked by a greater degree of finish and monumentality: their heads are larger in scale, their bodies less elongated and more firmly modelled'.[13] Conceptually, the two series are very similar, save that for Butts *Satan's and Raphael's Entries into Paradise* was replaced by *Adam and Eve Sleeping*. The latter is in every way a more successful composition, the former being too fragmented by the enormous V of cloud that divides Raphael from the serpent-entwined Satan on the left and the blissfully ignorant Adam and Eve on the right.

Blake plunges, as Milton does, *in medias res*. *Satan calling up his Legions* may portray, in the words of *The Marriage*, 'the Antediluvians who are our Energies',[14] but they are now seen as energies perverted by the will-to-power, as represented by the shield and spears in the right background. Satan is pseudo-heroic— Blake did not need modern criticism to tell him that the

Satan of the first two chapters of *Paradise Lost* is not to be taken at his own evaluation. *Satan Comes to the Gates of Hell* continues this pseudo-heroic theme, with the armed Satan confronting the adversary, Death, who is soon to become his ally. The rendering of Death as a transparent outline of a man is a more successful solution to the problem of picturing the unpicturable than had been found by Hogarth, Barry, or Fuseli in their compositionally similar treatments of this theme. *Christ Offers To Redeem Man* introduces a theme particularly close to Blake's interests, but here he has not entirely succeeded in bringing a feeling of conviction to the sorrowful paternal embrace, which forms the dramatic centre of this picture. The Father on his block-like throne seems too much like Urizen pawing Ahania—it may be simply that Blake had difficulty in rendering a doctrine—that of the Vicarious Atonement—which he deplored.

With *Satan Watching Adam and Eve* (*Pl.* 60), he is, in contrast, in an imaginative world fully credible. Adam and Eve embrace embowered by flowers in the night of Beulah, that earthly paradise in which, for a time, contraries are equally true. Above them flies Satan, his human self in an almost masturbatory relationship with his serpent self. This brilliant contrast did not occur to Blake immediately. There is in the Fogg Museum a drawing of this subject in which Satan merely holds his hands to his head in jealous dismay and the serpent slithers under the feet of the human lovers. *Adam and Eve Sleeping* presents another Beulah scene, but the toad Satan is already at Eve's ear. This sequence of lush scenes closes with *Raphael Warns Adam and Eve*.

The Casting of the Rebel Angels into Hell brings us into the retrospective account of war in heaven in Book VI. In a magnificent design, Christ in the orb of the sun bends a mighty bow, propelling Satan and his crew downward. Again we are reminded of how symbols are defined by their context in Blake's works. The bow is often associated with repressive morality, as in plate 35 of *Jerusalem*. With the black bow, Satan rent Moral Law from the Gospel, 'And spill'd the blood of mercy's Lord' in *Jerusalem*, plate 52.[15] But Christ's bow is like the intellectual bow wielded by Blake himself:

Los flam'd in my path & the Sun was hot
With the bows of my Mind & the Arrows of
　　Thought—
My bowstring fierce with Ardour breathes,
My arrows glow in their golden sheaves[16]

Another favourite conception of Blake's, though in this case not one peculiar to him, is seen in *The Creation of Eve* (*Pl.* 59). Typically, Eve would be created by the Father, as in Genesis. But to Blake the creation of woman was an act of sublime mercy accomplished by the Son, and he pictures it again in this way in *Jerusalem*, plate 31. There exists a pictorial tradition in which Jesus is shown creating Eve, as for example in the *Biblia Pauperum*. Blake chose to follow this tradition, investing it with his own particular meaning. He also makes Jesus rather than the Father the judge of Adam and Eve, after Eve, in an unusually sensuous evocation of the temptation and fall, has taken the apple from the serpent's mouth into her own (in Milton's text she plucks it from the tree). But Sin and Death, who do their worst at the top of *The Judgment of Adam and Eve*, collapse to the bottom of the Cross in *Michael Foretelling the Crucifixion*. The last design closely follows Milton's prose Argument, 'Michael in either hand leads them out of Paradise, the fiery sword waving behind them, and the Cherubim taking their stations to guard the place.'

Blake had long been interested in the *Hymn on the Morning of Christ's Nativity*, as is demonstrated by his imitation of its first three lines in *Europe* 3: 1–3,[17] and he must have welcomed the opportunity to become the only artist of his time to illustrate the poem comprehensively.[18] In the centre of the first of his six designs for this poem, he repeats the basic composition of his tempera *Nativity*, with the infant Jesus once more leaping forth in heavenly radiance. Next, he realizes in magnificent visual terms lines 109–16, where in 'A Globe of circular light'

The helmed Cherubim
And sworded Seraphim
　Are seen in glittering ranks with wings displayed.

But although Blake's angels play musical instruments as Milton's do, they bear no weapons. The Gothic manger of the preceding design is still faintly visible beneath the radiant orb. Then, in a cinematic effect, the manger is seen against a night sky in the third illustration, but the main picture space is taken up by demonic forms, and particularly 'Th' old Dragon underground', who 'Swinges the scaly Horror of his folded tail'. Blake has identified this Dragon with the seven-headed beast of Revelation in the Butts design (the earlier version has a six-headed dragon). Illustration 4 (*Pl.* 63) is perhaps the most interesting of the series, as it is an artistic polemic as well. The scene is indeed that of stanza XIX, showing the oracle at Delphos with a wild-looking Pythoness in a cave and, in the Thomas version only, a 'pale-eyed Priest'. But the Apollo of the Butts version is Apollo Belvedere (in the earlier Thomas version he holds the python instead of a bow), and his overthrow is the overthrow of the Neoclassical ideal which, as we have seen, Blake had come to consider incompatible with Christian art. Design 5 exorcizes Moloch, as the Christ child walks unharmed through the flames. In the last design we return to the manger, where the Virgin and child sleep guarded by angels.

Paradise Regained is the only Milton series of which Thomas Butts did not own a set, and it may be that the twelve pictures were executed for him but refused. It was William Michael Rossetti's opinion that 'Blake has here been less inspired than usual, and the result comparatively tame'.[19] It is difficult not to agree. There is something about the comparative largeness of the figures combined with the frequently static relations between or among them, that gives the series a feeling of passivity and even heaviness. Also, although this may in a sense be unfair to Blake, one cannot help recognizing themes in *Paradise Regained* that he managed more successfully elsewhere. *The Baptism of Christ* seems crowded and busy compared to the tempera of about 1799 (*Pl.* 75). *Satan Addressing His Potentates* demands comparison with both versions of its *Paradise Lost* counterpart, and it is simply a less powerful treatment of the subject, with the exception of the expressively conveyed despair in Satan's countenance. In *Angels Ministering to Christ*, one can see that Blake's intention is to create a sublimely serene Christ figure, and it may be that had he attempted this in the more uncompro-

misingly linear style of a few years earlier the result would have been more interesting. It is hard, however, to reconcile the rather full-bodied Christ figures of *Paradise Regained* with the deliberately anti-naturalistic situations Blake has invented.

This is not, of course, to say that all the *Paradise Regained* designs are failures. *Christ Tempted by Satan to Turn the Stones Into Bread* (*Pl.* 62) is particularly interesting. Satan as 'an aged man in rural weeds' (1: 314) seems genuinely perplexed as Jesus responds by pointing upwards after Satan has pointed down to the stone. Blake worked this episode into the symbolism of *Jerusalem*, where Albion's Spectre proclaims himself 'Bacon & Newton & Locke' and says

'Where is that Friend of Sinners? that Rebel
    against my Laws
'Who teaches Belief to the Nations & an unknown
    Eternal Life?
'Come hither into the Desart & turn these stones
    to bread.'

54: 19–21[20]

Yet when virtually this same composition is repeated in *Satan Tempts Christ with the Kingdoms of the Earth*, Christ seems to be too stolidly planted on his rock, conveying not the peace that passeth understanding, but an unexpressive passivity.

Perhaps the liveliest of Blake's Milton pictures are those for *L'Allegro* and *Il Penseroso*. At times these designs can appear cluttered, as if Blake has tried to pack too much meaning into too small a space, but on the whole they have a delightful sense of colour and free play of movement notably absent in *Paradise Regained*. Illustration 1, *Mirth*, also executed as an engraving (*Pl.* 61), has a covert meaning. The nymph is indeed lovely, owing something to Parmigianino's *Madonna of the Long Neck*, but Blake really takes a dim view of 'Quips and Cranks and wanton Wiles, Nods and Becks and wreathed Smiles', and a close consideration of the picture brings this out. *The Lark* is related to the Lark of *Milton a Poem*, 'Los's Messenger'.[21] *The Great Sun*, an Apollo-like figure imposing in his flaming disc, is perhaps to be contrasted with 'the more bright Sun of Imagination'[22] of 6. *A Sunshine Holiday* is one of the most beautiful pictures in the series; Blake says, in his programme notes, 'Mountains, Clouds, Rivers, Trees appear Humanized . . .'[23] The festivities in the lower part are reminiscent of 'The Ecchoing Green', but the female mountain in the upper centre does not seem to share the general joy, perhaps because according to Milton's text her breast is 'barren'. No. 5, *The Goblin*, introduces an element of whimsical fantasy with its depiction of 'the lubber fiend'. The first series ends with the image of *The Youthful Poet* attended by the spirits of Shakespeare and Jonson; still immature, he is writing in his sleep—i.e., according to literary models, and is to be contrasted with the vatic Milton of no. 12.

Il Penseroso begins with *Melancholy*, a superhuman-sized 'pensive Nun' admired by a diminutive poet-figure. This pursuit of false convention continues in *Milton and the Moon*, where the poet in undergraduate's cap and gown gazes at Cynthia (whose other mani-festations, we should remember, are Diana and Hecate). *Milton and the Spirit of Plato* (*Pl.* 57) is full of visual-symbolic clues as to why Milton, like some critics of Blake, is learning the wrong lesson from Plato and 'thrice great Hermes' (see Notes to the Plates). *Milton Led by Melancholy* shows the poet escaping from the 'flar-ing beams' of the sun, at best a strategic retreat into sleep. In *Milton's Dream*, as Damon points out,[24] Milton's crossed hands suggest repression; yet the 'strange mysterious dream' brings him materials for poetry. 'Around Milton', Blake writes, 'are Six Spirits or Fairies, hovering on the air, with Instruments of Music'.[25] This is a hopeful sign, preparing us for the vatic Milton of *Milton in his Old Age* (*Pl.* 58), whose extended arms open a space for the Imagination, as he 'bursts forth into a rapturous Prophetic Strain'. Thus Blake turned his *Il Penseroso* series into a spiritual history of the poet closest to his own imagination.

9. Till We Have Built Jerusalem

IN 1810 BLAKE closed his disastrous personal exhibition at his brother James's hosiery shop. He had attempted to appeal to the public directly, had written a *Descriptive Catalogue* setting forth his ideas about art, and had exhibited a range of his work from some of his earliest attempts to the recently completed *The spiritual form of Nelson guiding Leviathan* (*Pl.* 47) and *The spiritual form of Pitt, guiding Behemoth* (*Pl.* 48). In these two paintings of dead 'heroes', he had tried to establish a new type of history painting, one in which the subject would be not the Corporeal Acts of the hero but the divine pattern underlying those acts. But the exhibition had passed virtually unnoticed, save for a savage attack in the *Examiner*, in which Blake was described as 'an unfortunate lunatic'. At first Blake's impulse was to make yet another foray into the public realm, and he began working on an essay for this purpose in his *Notebook*. But in the end he did not do this. Instead, he concentrated his energies inwards, on painting and drawing, and on the completion of his epic poem, his ultimate work of composite art, *Jerusalem*.*

Jerusalem, like *Milton*, bears the date 1804 on its title-page. It was evidently in existence in some form in 1811, for Robert Southey reported seeing it in that year,[1] and in 1812 Blake showed at the Water Colour Society 'Detached Specimens of an original illuminated Poem, entitled 'Jerusalem . . .'[2] No extant copy, on the evidence of watermarks, can have been printed before 1818, no complete copy before 1820. The last copy known to have been published by Blake has some 1826 watermarks. Blake seems to have worked on *Jerusalem* over a period of about eighteen years until it could be issued as a work of four chapters, one hundred plates in all.

It is of course impossible in the scope of the present work to do justice to *Jerusalem*. What we can do is to give the reader the end of the golden string that winds into a ball, hoping that it will lead him 'in at Heaven's gate/ Built in Jerusalem's wall'. Perhaps we can best do this by a procedure which may seem arbitrary, but which at least has as its basis the structure Blake set up himself. Only three of the one hundred pages of *Jerusalem* are without recognizable decoration, but of the 97 designs, twelve occupy predetermined positions: each of the four chapters begins and ends with a design occupying part of a page, and each is followed by a full-page design. If we add to these twelve the two remaining full-page plates—the frontispiece and title-page—we have a selection of designs which Blake himself chose for emphasis. A discussion of these should serve as the end of that golden string.

The frontispiece (*Pl.* 96) shows Los as a watchman entering the Gothic doorway of the grave. He carries the lamp of Imagination, and the wind from the mausoleum blows his garments backward, to show that like Milton he descends against the current of Nature. (Contrast the old man of *Death's Door*, *Pls.* 45 and 46, whom the wind blows towards a natural death.) Los is like the sage in Plato's myth, voluntarily returning to the grave to bring truth to the bound captives. He is garbed as an eighteenth-century watchman, save for the sandal on his left foot, very recognizable in copy E. His dress is also much like Blake's own as it was described by the young artists who knew him in his later years: he tended to dress in black and to wear a broad-brimmed hat. In plate 56 of *Jerusalem* Los calls himself 'Albion's Watchman', and in plates 85–6 he sings his Watch Song. Near the culmination of *Jerusalem*, having accomplished his heroic task, he sheds his sombre garments to dance naked on plate 97, still holding his globe of fire, in the radiance of Eternity.

The title-page of *Jerusalem* (*Pl.* 97) serves as a good example of the problems which can exist in interpreting Blake's designs. Damon identifies the figures as 'Five of the Daughters of Beulah',[3] but Joseph Wicksteed sees those at the right and front centre as 'VALA . . . saved by JERUSALEM', the sitting figure as Beulah or Lambeth or Enitharmon, and the golden moth at the top as Erin.[4] Erdman also regards the butterfly-winged

---

* The single plate *On Homer's Poetry/ On Virgil* was issued about 1820; *The Ghost of Abel*, consisting of the two plates, bears the date 1822. These two slight works *may* post-date the completed *Jerusalem*.

sleeper as Jerusalem but sees the figure at the left as Vala.[5] The assumption is that each of these figures is a representation of a character in the poem and that the meaning of the plate is to be unravelled by reference to the text elsewhere. Sometimes such an approach works well, but here and at some other times it does not. The figures in the title-page design are not the major characters of the poem but belong to another order of being. They are Fairies, mentioned in plate 3 of *Jerusalem* and referred to in the *Descriptive Catalogue* as 'the rulers of the vegetable world'. Unlike the Daughters of Beulah, these presiding spirits of nature are insect-winged, as we know from the *Notebook* poem called 'The Fairy': 'Let him laugh, let him cry,/ He's my butter-fly'.[6] What the Fairies on the title-page are doing is miming the theme of *Jerusalem*—the sleep of death, the lamentation over it, the soaring hope of regeneration from it. The design does not illustrate an episode; it is a parallel thematic statement.

Chapter 1 is introduced by a design which again has no specific textual reference, though there the participants can be identified by name. The naked woman at the left and the cowled one in the centre are Jerusalem and Vala, as they are also depicted on plate 46. Jerusalem leads the daughters of Albion toward the moon of Beulah, across the dark part of which is written in Greek Μονος ὁ Ιεσους ('Jesus alone'). While the naked Jerusalem leads the girls of England to freedom, the lower world under the dividing cloud is presided over by Vala. This world below is England's green and pleasant land, with the sea of time and space beating against the cliffs of Dover. Vala has a firm grip on the son of Albion at her left, but the one at the right seems to be escaping her grasp to pray to (or dive after?) the ascending children of Jerusalem. (Cf. the sibylline instruction in *America*, plate 14, where the youth's worshipful gesture is directed towards rather than away from the Vala-figure.)

Plate 25 (*Pl.* 104), one of the most disturbing in Blake's oeuvre, closes Chapter 1. The central figure is very similar to the victim in the Butts watercolour *The Blasphemer*, but his tormentors are not men as in that picture but three terrible women: the whore Rahab, whose gaze hypnotically enchants Albion at the left;

the virgin Tirzah, who disembowels him at the right; and Vala, hovering cruciform behind, with fibres of vegetation emanating from her downturned hands. These fibres are the same as those being wound out of Albion's navel, the basic stuff of natural existence. The design as a whole shows Blake's remarkable ability to conflate visual sources. The women were originally envisaged standing up, as studies in the collections of the Fogg Museum (*Pl.* 105) and of Sir Geoffrey Keynes show. But then Blake altered the positions of the women to resemble those of the three Fates in an anonymous engraving after Il Rosso Fiorentino, greatly intensifying the dramatic situation.[7] The conception of the disembowelled Albion Blake borrowed from *The Martyrdom of St Erasmus* by Poussin, which had been engraved by Joseph Marie Mitelli.

The full-page design which concludes Chapter 1 shows the giant Hand in flames, demonically parodying Christ even to the point of displaying stigmata. The flames form a false halo around his head and elongate into a serpent over his cruciform arms. This false Christ is regarded with horror by Jerusalem. Exactly fifty plates later comes the visionary contrary of this design. Plate 76 shows Albion imitating Christ, crucified on the Tree of Mystery, as the first gleams of dawn appear in the east. Here Albion's attitude signifies the death of the Selfhood which is true freedom, linking him to the engraving *Albion rose* and 'the dance of Eternal Death'.

The head-piece to Chapter 2 (*Pl.* 103) is one of the most controversial designs in *Jerusalem*. Two figures embrace in a water-lily, evidently the 'Lilly of Havilah' of plate 19 (a reference to Genesis—'the whole land of Havilah, where there is gold'). If we take the picture to relate to the text of plate 19, then the two figures must be Jerusalem and Vala—spirit and body locked in a lesbian embrace. There is, however, another passage, on plate 20, to which the picture may refer. This describes the primal sexual act which ultimately resulted in Albion's guilt-ridden rejection of Eros. 'When', as Jerusalem recalls to Vala, 'Albion rent thy beautiful net of gold and silver twine.' In that case, we would have Albion and Vala copulating in the flower in plate 28. There is a previous state of the plate (*Pl.* 102) in which the two figures can be assumed to be copulating.[8] Blake turned the legs side-saddle in the second state so that this could no longer be the case, and he also expunged the rather tumid caterpillar—another sexual reference, as in *The Gates of Paradise*. There also exists an intermediate state of plate 28 (in the Morgan Library), where the figures' legs have been redrawn (not etched) so as to change them from the initial position to the final one, and the caterpillar's ghost is distinctly visible. Whatever the reason for these changes, it is notable that the two figures even in the revised state suggest a single amalgamated being, like one of the creatures of Aristophanes' parable in *The Symposium*. This is reinforced by their features, which if looked at carefully seem to form a single face. Here again is a reminder of the unfallen composite sexuality which humanity possessed in Eden.

Chapter 2 ends with the horrifying true figure of Hand, who, having cast off his Christ-like disguise, sits on the cliffs of Dover as the sea breaks before him. He is triple-headed like Dante's Satan, and this image on plate 50 is elaborated in the text of 70, where the other Sons of Albion are described as issuing from his key-bones and chest. Still another aspect of Hand was once intended for plate 51, where, as a preliminary drawing indicates (*Pl.* 106), he would have been a baboon-like monster. In the etched version, however, only three figures appear (*Pl.* 107), their names given on a separate print as Vala, Hyle, and Skofield. Vala wears the spiked crown of dominion and bears in her right hand a sceptre tipped with the fleur-de-lys, a symbol of the *ancien régime* which had been adopted by Napoleon. Hyle, whose name signifies matter in Greek and is also suggestive of Hayley, sits in utter despair. Skofield, his head shaven, and wearing manacles and chains, is suffering appropriately for having accused Blake of seditious utterances in 1803. He corresponds, as already noted, to Despair in *The House of Death*. These are, as St Paul calls them in a passage quoted by Blake on the title-page of *The Four Zoas*, 'the blind world-rulers of this life',[9] revealed in their true spiritual condition.

The design which begins Chapter 3 shows yet another figure in a flower, a diminutive nature-goddess wearing the papal tiara, her butterfly wings forming a sort of throne that blocks off the radiance of the sun behind

her. This design may be compared to Dante illustration 99, where the Queen of Heaven, bearing a fleur-de-lys sceptre in one hand and a looking-glass in the other, incarnates the Female Will in all its narcissism and striving for dominion. On plate 75, a related being closes this chapter. She is Rahab, seen here in front and back views, amalgamating with the seven-headed beast. Here the design relates closely to the text on the same page: 'thus Rahab is reveal'd,/ Mystery, Babylon the Great, the Abomination of Desolation'.[10] This is of course one of Blake's favourite themes: an epitome of State and Church as pictured in *Night Thoughts* VIII, already discussed (*Pl.* 35) and in Dante illustration 89. In *Jerusalem* 75 (*Pl.* 99), however, there is a redemptive sign—the frieze of angels traversing the upper third of the page. These offer an alternative to the nightmare of cyclical recurrence epitomized in the amalgamated Rahab-dragon.

After Albion's imitation of Christ we begin the fourth and last chapter, with a disconsolate-looking bird-headed man seated on the cliffs of Dover. This composite creature has the crest of a cock and the beak of a vulture; he seems to be derived from the animal-headed gods of Egypt, and in that case would represent debased humanity, as does the equally enigmatic swan-woman of plate 11. But regeneration is at hand; Albion rises in 95 (*Pl.* 100), and in 99 the Universal Father embraces the soul amid the flames of the Last Judgment. In plate 100 (*Pl.* 101), Los stands in naked majesty with his hammer and tongs while the Spectre of Urthona bears the sun away on its daily round. On the right, Enitharmon with her shuttle continues her weaving—it seems that bodies are still going to be necessary after all, and her fibres descend to the crescent moon and then down to the earth. Behind them all is a version of the Serpent Temple at Avebury as 'restored' in the engravings of William Stukeley. The Druid temple, too, has its unfallen form, but there may also be another meaning here. Plate 100 seems, in contrast to the text on plates 95–9, decidedly unapocalyptic. It looks as if the arts of life are about to recommence rather than disappear, and if that is so, then the design on plate 100 provides an alternative ending for *Jerusalem*, though each ending is optimistic in its own way.

10. The Traveller Hasteth in the Evening

BLAKE DID NOT ENTIRELY sink from view after 1810, but it is clear that he gave up any further attempt to realize his public ambitions. He did continue to work both as an artist and as a poet, and he continued to engrave after other artists (the 37 Hesiod engravings after Flaxman date from about 1814, and Blake was working on the Sculpture plates for Rees's *Cyclopaedia* in 1815). All the while, of course, he was finishing *Jerusalem.* In addition to that great work, his important productions of the last decade of his life consist of series of designs on four subjects, two minor and two major: illustrations to *The Pilgrim's Progress*, to Virgil's *Eclogues*, to *The Book of Job*, and to *The Divine Comedy.* The Dante and *Job* projects came about as a result of Blake's association with John Linnell, who enabled him to live his last years without fear of starvation, in addition to making possible the conditions in which some of his greatest works were produced.

The genesis of the *Pilgrim's Progress* designs is unclear. It is true that Blake always had some interest in Bunyan, albeit his sympathy was tempered by the rigidity of Bunyan's allegory. His *Gates of Paradise* engraving *The Traveller hasteth in the Evening* seems inspired by *The Pilgrim's Progress*, and in a letter to Hayley he applies Bunyan's words to himself: 'I shall travel on in the strength of the Lord God, as Poor Pilgrim says'. One does not know what to make of his analogy in another letter: a collaboration with Flaxman would be '(to say the best of myself) like putting John Milton with John Bunyan',[1] for it is hard to imagine Blake believing Flaxman to be so far above him. 'Fable or Allegory', he writes in his *Notebook*, 'is seldom without some vision. *Pilgrim's Progress* is full of it . . .'[2] The underlying vision would have to be extracted from the fable or allegory like the seed from its husk. This is no doubt what Blake intended to do in the series of illustrations, but he succeeded only to a limited extent, if only because some of the pictures were not finished. The designs are intensely colourful, but they suffer at times from the same heaviness as is found in the *Paradise Regained* pictures. Curiously, no such constraint is found in

another Bunyan subject—*The Man Sweeping the Interpreter's Parlour* (*Pl.* 92), issued in a second state about this time. (Blake's young friends the 'Ancients' called his rooms 'The Interpreter's Parlour', and so the subject may have had a warm personal significance for Blake.) Still, some of the *Pilgrim's Progress* designs are undoubtedly powerful—*Christian reading in his Book*, for example—and *Christian beaten down by Apollyon* (*Pl.* 93) is a magnificent piece of grotesquerie.

The illustrations for Robert John Thornton's *Pastorals* of Virgil promised less and delivered more. They were commissioned in 1820 for a schoolbook; Blake had not executed wood engravings before, and Dr Thornton was not pleased with the results. Yet these beautiful gems of book illustration (*Fig.* 10) are among Blake's triumphs. No one has done them more justice than Samuel Palmer, whose work, along with Edward Calvert's, was much influenced by them: 'They are visions of little dells, and nooks, and corners of Paradise.'[3]

Yet undeniably the two great achievements of Blake's later years are the illustrations to *Job* and to Dante. He had long been interested in the story of Job, as attested by his pen and wash drawing of about 1785, his early line engraving, and his tempera *Job and His Daughters* (*Pl.* 109). The date and circumstances of the creation of the great watercolour series for Thomas Butts are not clear: Gilchrist placed them in 1821, but this date has recently been questioned on stylistic grounds, and an earlier one of about 1805–10 suggested.[4] In 1821, at the instigation of John Linnell, these designs were borrowed back and a second set of watercolours was produced for Linnell. In 1823, Blake and Linnell made up a Memorandum of Agreement in which Blake undertook to engrave the series with Linnell acting as his publisher and employer. The first pulls were taken in 1825 and the series published as *Illustrations of the Book of Job* in 1826. In this series Blake achieved his greatest success in the art of engraving, combining intimacy with monumentality in a manner unique to him. He had assimilated the styles of 'the old original

FIG. 10 *Illustrations for Robert John Thornton's 'Pastorals' of Virgil: Imitation of Eclogue I*, nos. 2–5. 1820–1. Wood engraving. Design area of each block measures approximately 1⅜ × 2⅞ in. London, British Museum

Engravers' at last, and at the same time he had introduced a quality of his own, the sort of attraction that, as Gaston Bachelard says, makes us desire to live in an engraving.

The *Job* series was one of the first extended Blakean symbolisms to be understood, thanks to Joseph Wicksteed's *Blake's Vision of the Book of Job*, first published in 1910. Wicksteed showed that *Job* utilized a fairly consistent symbolism of right and left in which the stage-

right (our left) suggested the spiritual and the stage-left (our right) the material (the meanings attached to the right and left in traditional Last Judgments).[5] This method of interpretation works fairly well if we do not use it too remorselessly and if we bear in mind that it does not necessarily apply to Blake's other works. Thus when Job gives charity in plate 5, he gives it with his left hand, showing that he is observing the letter of the law but not informed by its spirit. Of course some of the designs make their point without such iconography; it takes no private knowledge to see that in plate 1, *Thus did Job continually* (*Pl.* 110), there is something wrong with the situation in which everyone prays dutifully while the instruments of music hang unused on the tree. In plate 21, *So the Lord blessed the latter end of Job more than the beginning* (*Pl.* 111), the entire Job family greets the sunrise with music. Other designs have a special meaning for Blake, as *Behold now Behemoth which I made with thee* (*Pl.* 108), where the two monsters in the terraqueous globe still bear some of their meaning from the *Pitt* and *Nelson* paintings; but now, seen from a divine perspective, they are not so much apocalyptic forces as unusual household pets. This type of symbolism has always drawn new admirers to Blake, for it 'rouzes the faculties to act'.

Although interpretations may differ as to details, the overall meaning of Blake's *Job* is clear. Job is a man who trusts in moral virtue, and as this is external, so Job is attacked in externals. The God whom Job has created in his own image will allow Satan, the lord of this world, to deprive Job of everything except his life. He emanations, his sons and daughters, are taken from him; like the sin-obsessed Albion of *Jerusalem*, he is afflicted with boils. His three false comforters are actually accusers of sin, and in plate 10 of *Job* they make the pointing gesture of the triple accuser in plate 93 of *Jerusalem*. At night he is visited by terrifying visions (plate 11) of a cloven-hoofed, serpent-entwined God in a composition reminiscent of the colour print *Elohim Creating Adam* (*Pl.* 28). The turning point comes in the next plate, where Elihu reproves both Job and the comforters. Some commentators, misled by Elihu's gesture towards the stars, have interpreted his message as a Deistic one—an appeal to God's manifestation in the natural order of things. It is true that Blake would have rejected such a view as vehemently as he rejected the moralism of Bildad, Zophar, and Eliphaz; but neither in the Old Testament text nor in Blake's design is this the burden of the meaning. 'Against Job was his wrath kindled, because he justified himself rather than God. Also against his three friends was his wrath kindled, because they had found no answer, and yet had condemned Job.' (32:2–3). To confirm this view of Elihu as a positive force, we need only examine the marginal designs of plate 12. All through the series the marginal designs have thematic importance—those of the several preceding plates have been strongly negative in character: flames, bat wings, chains, briars, toadstools, and the like. Now suddenly we come to a horde of little figures flying upward on both sides and converging among the stars at the top centre. These fairy forms emanate from a sleeping Job-figure who lies with his left hand on a scroll in the bottom centre. Job is still spiritually asleep, but Elihu's words have liberated his imagination, and thoughts of which he is as yet unconscious rise at the direction of two angelic beings in the lower left-hand corner.

This episode is immediately followed by God speaking to Job from the whirlwind. God is no longer the static patriarch imagined by Job in plates 2 and 5: he is a sublimely powerful figure who flies cruciform in the midst of a whirling vortex of energy. The three friends hide their heads before this vision but Job and his wife face it in prayer. As a result, the forces of the Creation are revealed in plate 14, one of Blake's most famous designs, 'When the morning Stars sang together, & all the Sons of God shouted for joy'. Now all of nature is seen from a visionary perspective, much as it is in *Milton*. In the lower margin, as if to counterbalance the frieze of angels in the upper part of the design, are Leviathan and the coiled worm of mortality; but by being placed in another dimension of visual reality, these forces are shown to be illusory, a theme enlarged upon in 'Behold now Behemoth which I made with thee', plate 15. Job has lived out the dialectic that underlies all Blake's later works, beginning in a state of innocence (which would, however, become stagnant if artificially prolonged), passing through the agonies of

experience in which all things are put to question, to emerge as a regenerate being after experiencing the divine vision. Consequently, Satan is cast out in plate 16, which in Blake's terms means that error has been defined and rejected: Job has purged himself of the utilitarian morality and adherence to moral law which governed his actions in plates 1, 2, and 5. God now appears to him in radiant human form (plate 17), as if fulfilling the words of Jesus in *Jerusalem*—'I am not a God afar off, I am a brother and friend.'[6] As the image of this true God, Job assumes a cruciform posture in plate 18, 'And my Servant Job shall pray for you'. He is now the thankful receiver of charity in plate 19, a design replete with images of fertility: the fig tree overhead, the field of wheat in the background, the palms of victory in the margins. Having regained his emanations, he is seen with his daughters in plate 20, where he inhabits a place similar to Los's halls in *Milton*, where the archetypal configurations of human experience—in this instance Job's own experience—are represented. 'So the Lord blessed the latter end of Job more than the beginning' (plate 21).

Having fostered a masterpiece in *Job*, John Linnell attempted to do the same with Dante, and in 1824 Blake began to illustrate *The Divine Comedy*. According to tradition, the corner of Hampstead Heath near Linnell's house at North End became known to children as Dante's Wood, because Blake used to sketch at Collins' Farm, as it was then called, when he visited the Linnells there. From 1824 until his death in August 1827, Blake worked on the Dante pictures, producing 102 large drawings and several smaller ones, varying in degree of finish from highly worked-up watercolours to slight pencil sketches. Of these Blake lived to engrave only seven, including the magnificent *Whirlwind of Lovers* (*Pl.* 116), in which Paolo and Francesca's pathos in isolation is brilliantly conveyed. These drawings and engravings show Blake at the height of his powers and among them are found some of his most successful designs. However, there is an essential difference between the Dante series and a series like *Job* or *Paradise Lost*. In the two latter, Blake felt an intuitive sympathy with his subject and in his illustrative interpretation he tried to recreate what he saw as the underlying

Portrait of
Mr Blake — 1825   J L. f. ...

meaning of the work. He felt no such sympathy for Dante. In annotating Henry Boyd's *Historical Notes on Dante* around 1800, Blake had written 'Dante gives too much Caesar: he is not a Republican.'[7] Now, although he had learned enough Italian to read the original, his vehemence against Dante only increased. On the back of his seventh drawing he wrote, 'Every thing in Dante's Comedia shews that for Tyrannical Purposes he has made This World the Foundation of All, & the Goddess Nature Memory is his Inspirer & not Imagination the Holy Ghost.'[8] Just as he could not accept Swedenborg's Hell, Blake could not accept Dante's. Therefore the Dante series, despite its strength and scope, does not have a firm, unified structure: it hardly matters, for example, whether we are in Hell, Purgatory, or Paradise as far as Blake is concerned; the designs provide their own contexts of meaning, drawing upon the iconographic vocabulary of Blake's later works.[9]

Of the large drawings, 69 are designated for the *Inferno*, 19 for the *Purgatorio*, and 9 for the *Paradiso*; and of the three lacking canto numbers, two are evidently for the *Inferno*. This preponderance of the imagery of Hell is not difficult to explain, for although Blake asserted that 'He [God] could never have built Dante's Hell',[10] the artist could find there a wealth of correspondences to life on earth. Thus when Virgil leads Dante forward in *The Inscription Over the Gate*, Dante is like Thel passing the northern bar or the Soul exploring the recesses of the Grave. The monstrous creatures encountered in Hell are, like the 'Ruin'd Spirits' of *The Four Zoas*, 'dishumaniz'd men'.[11] The figures who are bitten by and then turn into serpents, for example, are simply revealing their true natures as in *Agnolo Brunelleschi and the Six-Footed Serpent* (Pl. 114). Sometimes we encounter figures familiar from other works, such as the mighty hunter Nimrod (Pl. 115) of *Jerusalem*, plate 61 (see Notes to the Plates). The lightly sketched *Ugolino in Prison* repeats the composition of plate 12 of *The Gates of Paradise* (Fig. 5) and plate 16 of *The Marriage of Heaven and Hell*, but the Dante drawing adds

two hovering angels which also appear in the tempera *Ugolino in Prison* of 1827. What Blake says of Fuseli's Ugolino he might also say of his own:[12] Ugolino is a man displaying 'passionate and innocent grief . . . innocent and venerable madness and insanity and fury . . .' This imposition of Blake's characteristic meanings upon Dante's poem continues in Purgatory, where, as if to show the mistaken nature of Dante's belief, the sun is always either occluded,[13] setting, or absent. The angel guarding the entrance is decidedly Urizenic, as is his act of marking Dante with the signs of the Seven Deadly Sins. The poets ascend a path hewn out of rock over the Sea of Time and Space, and in *The Rock Sculptured with the Recovery of the Ark and the Annunciation* (Pl. 113) they are rewarded with visions of archetypal art, much like those 'bright Sculptures of/ Los's Halls' in plate 16 of *Jerusalem*.[14] Yet their entire quest is, from Blake's perspective, erroneous. The climactic appearance of Beatrice in the chariot of the Church, representing to Dante the miracle of the Eucharist, is for Blake a manifestation of Vala as ruler of Dante's universe. Despite its intense beauty, *Beatrice Addressing Dante from the Car* (Pl. 112) signifies the poet's submission to the delusive goddess Nature. Even in Paradise Blake finds this illusion: *The Queen of Heaven in Glory* depicts the Virgin holding in one hand an imperial fleur-de-lys and in the other the looking-glass of this vegetable world. Blake resolved his quarrel with Milton by assimilating Milton's vision with his own; his quarrel with Dante could never be resolved.

Blake died on 12 August 1827, and on 17 August was buried in Bunhill Fields. He left behind him a body of work which amply fulfils the high goals he had set for himself:

> I rest not from my great task!
> To open the Eternal Worlds, to open the immortal Eyes
> Of Man inwards into the Worlds of Thought, into Eternity
> Ever expanding in the Bosom of God, the Human Imagination.
>
> *Jerusalem* 5: 17–20[15]

FIG. 11 (*opposite*) JOHN LINNELL: *William Blake*. 1820. Pencil. 7⅞ × 6⅛ in. (enlarged). Cambridge, Fitzwilliam Museum

Notes to the Text

Works frequently alluded to in the Notes are indicated by abbreviations as follows:

Keynes: *The Complete Writings of William Blake*, ed. Geoffrey Keynes. London, Oxford University Press, 1966.

Blake Records: *Blake Records*, ed. G. E. Bentley, Jr. Oxford, The Clarendon Press, 1969.

Bindman: David Bindman, *Blake as an Artist*. Oxford, Phaidon Press, 1977. Published in the U.S.A. by E. P. Dutton, New York, 1977.

Blunt: Anthony Blunt, *The Art of William Blake*. London, Oxford University Press, 1959.

Butlin: Martin Butlin, *William Blake: a Complete Catalogue of the Works in the Tate Gallery*. London, Tate Gallery, rev. ed. 1971.

Damon: S. Foster Damon, *William Blake: His Philosophy and Symbols*. Boston, Houghton Mifflin, 1924.

Blake Dictionary: S. Foster Damon, *A Blake Dictionary*. Providence, Brown University Press, 1965.

Prophet: David V. Erdman, *William Blake: Prophet Against Empire*. Garden City, N.Y., Doubleday & Co., rev. ed. 1969.

Illuminated Blake: *The Illuminated Blake*, ed. David V. Erdman. Garden City, N.Y., Doubleday & Co., 1974.

Todd: Alexander Gilchrist, *Life of William Blake* (2 vols., 1863), ed. Ruthven Todd. New York, E. P. Dutton, rev. ed. 1945.

Chapter 1

1. Todd, p. 4.
2. *Blake Records*, p. 510.
3. *Blake Records*, p. 511.
4. *Blake Records*, p. 606.
5. Keynes, p. 820.
6. The hard and fast distinction which we make between etching and engraving cannot be applied to plate-making in the late eighteenth and early nineteenth centuries, where a combination of both techniques was often used and either term applied.
7. See Sidney C. Hutchinson, *History of the Royal Academy 1768–1968*. London, Chapman and Hall, 1968, pp. 89–90, 115.
8. Todd, p. 12.
9. Todd, p. 14.
10. *Blake Records*, p. 422.
11. Geoffrey Keynes, *Engravings by William Blake: The Separate Plates*. Dublin, Emery Walker, 1956, pp. 3–5.
12. Keynes, p. 449.
13. Keynes, p. 457.
14. Geoffrey Grigson, 'Painters of the Abyss'. *Arch. Rev.*, CVIII (1950), p. 218.
15. See Blunt, pp. 6–7.
16. Keynes, p. 446.
17. See *Prophet*, pp. 38–45.
18. Keynes, p. 595.

19. See Ruthven Todd, 'Two Blake Prints and Two Fuseli Drawings'. *Blake Newsletter*, V (1971–2), pp. 173–81.
20. Keynes, p. 551.
21. *Blake Records*, p. 460.
22. Keynes, p. 62.
23. See Geoffrey Keynes, *Bibliography of William Blake*. New York, Grolier Club, 1921, p. 10.
24. R. N. Essick, 'William Blake as an Engraver and Etcher', in *William Blake in the Art of his Time*, exhibition catalogue, University of California, Santa Barbara Art Galleries, 1976, pp. 16–18.
25. See Ruthven Todd, 'The Techniques of William Blake's Illuminated Printing'. *Print Collector's Quarterly*, XXIX (1948), pp. 25–36.
26. See Essick, *op. cit.* and his forthcoming study of Blake's graphic art.
27. *Blake Records*, p. 460, n. 1.
28. See Geoffrey Keynes, bibliographical note to the facsimile edition of *There is No Natural Religion*, William Blake Trust, 1971.
29. Keynes, p. 781.
30. Keynes, p. 793.
31. *Illuminated Blake*, pp. 68–9.
32. *Illuminated Blake*, p. 44.
33. Blunt, p. 48.
34. See David V. Erdman, 'Dating Blake's Script: the "g" Hypothesis'. *Blake Newsletter*, III (1969), pp. 8–13.
35. See *William Blake: An Illustrated Catalogue of Works in the Fitzwilliam Museum, Cambridge*, ed. David Bindman. Cambridge, 1970, p. 8.
36. Keynes, p. 100.
37. See David Bindman, 'Blake's "Gothicised Imagination" and the History of England', in *William Blake: Essays in Honour of Sir Geoffrey Keynes*, eds. M. D. Paley and M. Phillips. Oxford, The Clarendon Press, 1973, pp. 29–49.
38. Keynes, p. 799.
39. Todd, pp. 46–7.
40. Keynes, p. 508.
41. Keynes, *Blake Studies: Essays on his Life and Work*, 2nd ed., Oxford, The Clarendon Press, 1971, p. 4.
42. Blunt, p. 2.
43. Here I do not refer to commercial engravings of which Blake was the designer as well as the engraver.

Chapter 2

1. Keynes, p. 91.
2. Keynes, pp. 131–3.
3. Keynes, p. 157.
4. See Robert Hindmarsh, *Rise and Progress of the New Jerusalem Church*. London, Hodson & Son, 1861, p. 142.

5. A similar design in 'The Ecchoing Green' of *Innocence* has a clearly positive meaning, but this may not be the case in *Marriage*, plate 2.
6. See Erdman, Dargan and Van Meter, 'Reading the Illuminations of Blake's *Marriage of Heaven and Hell*', in *William Blake: Essays in Honour of Sir Geoffrey Keynes*, pp. 162–207.
7. Keynes, p. 208.
8. Keynes, p. 172.
9. Keynes, p. 729.
10. Damon, p. 284.
11. Keynes, p. 179.
12. See *Prophet*, pp. 202–5.
13. Keynes, p. 97.
14. David V. Erdman with Donald K. Moore, *The Notebook of William Blake*. Oxford, The Clarendon Press, 1973, p. 9.
15. These are reproduced in the *Notebook*, with extensive discussion.
16. See Erdman, 'Blake's Vision of Slavery'. *JWCI*, XV (1952), pp. 242–52.
17. See Erdman in *Blake Newsletter*, IX (1976), p. 126.
18. Keynes, p. 196.
19. See Damon, pp. 339–41; Erdman, '*America*: New Expanses', in *Blake's Visionary Forms Dramatic*, eds. D. V. Erdman and J. E. Grant. Princeton, Princeton University Press, 1970, pp. 92–114.
20. *Illuminated Blake*, pp. 153–4.
21. Keynes, p. 233.
22. Keynes, p. 190.
23. Keynes, p. 156.
24. M. D. Paley, *Energy and the Imagination: a Study of the Development of Blake's Thought*. Oxford, The Clarendon Press, 1970, pp. 61–88.
25. *Prophet*, pp. 218–19.
26. Keynes, p. 305.
27. Keynes, p. 248.
28. Keynes, p. 383.

Chapter 3

1. Keynes, p. 867.
2. Cf. Keynes, p. 203.
3. Blunt, p. 34.
4. Keynes, p. 160.
5. Butlin, p. 34.
6. See Butlin, p. 35.
7. Keynes, p. 243.
8. Butlin, p. 34.
9. Keynes, p. 795.
10. Keynes, p. 233.
11. Keynes, p. 566.
12. Jean Hagstrum, 'Christ's Body', in *William Blake: Essays in Honour of Sir Geoffrey Keynes*, p. 150.

13. The date was formerly thought to be later, but **see** Mary K. Woodworth in *N & Q*, NS XVII (August 1970), pp. 312–13.
14. See Irene Tayler, *Blake's Illustrations to the Poems of Gray*. Princeton, Princeton University Press, 1971, pp. 55–70.
15. Keynes, p. 792.
16. Keynes, pp. 793–4.
17. Keynes, p. 795.

Chapter 4

1. *Blake Records*, pp. 78–9.
2. *Blake Records*, p. 82.
3. Todd, p. 140.
4. Keynes, p. 812.
5. Keynes, p. 544. Cf. Keynes, p. 6.
6. Keynes, p. 819.
7. Keynes, p. 486.
8. Keynes, p. 809.
9. Keynes, p. 814.
10. *Blake Records*, p. 571.
11. Keynes, p. 825.
12. Keynes, p. 825.
13. Keynes, p. 264.
14. Damon, p. 399; Keynes, p. 267.
15. *William Blake: Vala or the Four Zoas*, ed. G. E. Bentley, Jr. Oxford, The Clarendon Press, 1963, p. 183.

Chapter 5

1. *Blake Records*, pp. 168–9.
2. *Blake Records*, p. 195.
3. Keynes, p. 708.
4. Keynes, p. 442.
5. Harley MS. 4866. I owe this suggestion to Ms Betsy Bowden.
6. Keynes, p. 567.
7. Keynes, p. 572.
8. Keynes, p. 819.
9. Todd, p. 248.
10. Keynes, p. 586.
11. Keynes, p. 592.

Chapter 6

1. Keynes, p. 852.
2. Keynes, p. 564.
3. Keynes, p. 463.
4. Keynes, pp. 476–7.
5. Keynes, p. 457.
6. Keynes, p. 473.
7. Keynes, p. 459.

8. *Portraits of Sir Joshua Reynolds*, ed. F. W. Hilles. New Haven, Yale University Press, 1949, p. 148.
9. William Hazlitt, 'Character of Sir Joshua Reynolds'. *Essays on the Fine Arts*. London, Reeves and Turner, 1873, p. 31.
10. Keynes, p. 792. See Bindman, p. 126.
11. Keynes, pp. 814–5.
12. Keynes, pp. 582–3.
13. Keynes, p. 638.
14. Keynes, p. 565.
15. *Lectures on Painting by the Royal Academicians*, ed. Ralph N. Wornum. London, Bohn, 1848, pp. 57–73.
16. Keynes, p. 480.
17. Keynes, p. 792.
18. Keynes, p. 201.
19. Keynes, p. 798.
20. Keynes, p. 593.
21. Keynes, p. 600.
22. *Blake Records*, p. 238.

Chapter 7

1. See G. E. Bentley, Jr., 'Thomas Butts, White Collar Maecenas'. *PMLA*, LXXI (1956), pp. 1052–66.
2. Keynes, p. 795.
3. Bindman, pp. 126–7.
4. Keynes, p. 745.
5. Keynes, p. 814.
6. Keynes, p. 824.
7. M. Butlin, 'The Blake Collection of Mrs William T. Tonner'. *Bulletin/Philadelphia Museum of Art*, LXVII (1972), p. 18.
8. Keynes, pp. 604–17.
9. Keynes, pp. 442–4.
10. Keynes, p. 441.

Chapter 8

1. Keynes, p. 150.
2. Preface to *Prometheus Unbound. The Complete Poetical Works of Percy Bysshe Shelley*, ed. Thomas Hutchinson. London, Oxford University Press, 1956, p. 205.
3. Keynes, p. 506.
4. Keynes, p. 845.
5. Keynes, p. 823.
6. Keynes, p. 592.
7. Keynes, p. 481.
8. Keynes, p. 497.
9. Keynes, p. 505. (Cf. p. 818).
10. *Illuminated Blake*, p. 248.
11. Keynes, p. 741.
12. Keynes, p. 507.
13. M. Butlin, 'A "Minute Particular" Particularized'. *Blake Newsletter*, VI (1972), p. 46.

14. Keynes, p. 155.
15. Keynes, p. 683.
16. Keynes, p. 818.
17. Keynes, p. 239.
18. See Marcia R. Pointon, *Milton and English Art*. Manchester, Manchester University Press, 1970, p. 161.
19. As quoted in the Fitzwilliam Museum *William Blake* catalogue, p. 41, n. 1.
20. Keynes, p. 685.
21. Keynes, p. 526.
22. Keynes, p. 618.
23. Keynes, p. 618.
24. *Blake Dictionary*, p. 277.
25. Keynes, p. 619.

Chapter 9

1. *Blake Records*, p. 229.
2. *Blake Records*, p. 231.
3. Damon, p. 468.
4. Joseph Wicksteed, *William Blake's Jerusalem*. London, Blake Trust, 1954, pp. 109–10.
5. *Illuminated Blake*, pp. 282–3.
6. Keynes, p. 178.
7. See M. D. Paley and D. Toomey, 'Two Pictorial Sources for *Jerusalem 25*'. *Blake Newsletter*, V (1971–2), pp. 185–90.
8. See Erdman, 'The Suppressed and Altered Passages in Blake's *Jerusalem*'. *Studies in Bibliography*, XVII (1964), p. 1820. Also *Illuminated Blake*, p. 399.
9. Keynes, p. 263.
10. Keynes, p. 716.

Chapter 10

1. Keynes, pp. 853, 942.
2. Keynes, p. 604.
3. *Blake Records*, p. 271.
4. 1807–10 according to Bo Lindberg, *William Blake's Illustrations to the Book of Job*. Abo, Finland, Abo Akademi, 1973, p. 19. Butlin suggests they may be as early as 1805.
5. Damon, p. 225.
6. Keynes, p. 622.
7. Keynes, p. 413.
8. Keynes, p. 785.
9. See Albert S. Roe, *Blake's Illustrations to the Divine Comedy*. Princeton, Princeton University Press, 1953.
10. Keynes, p. 785.
11. Keynes, p. 314.
12. Keynes, p. 864.
13. Butlin, p. 72.
14. Keynes, p. 638.
15. Keynes, p. 623.

Chronology

1757	28 November: born at 28 Broad Street, Golden Square, Westminster		Mary Wollstonecraft: *Vindication of the Rights of Woman*
	11 December: baptized at St James's Church, Piccadilly	*c.* 1793	The History of England series
1767	Enrols at Henry Pars's drawing school	1793	21 January: Execution of Louis XVI
1772	4 August: is apprenticed to James Basire, engraver, for seven years		Godwin: *Political Justice*
			For Children: The Gates of Paradise
1779	8 October: is admitted to Royal Academy Schools as a full student		*Visions of the Daughters of Albion*
			28 January: preparation for war against France
1780	6 June: witnesses Gordon Riots	1793–4	*America, a Prophecy*
1782	18 August: marries Catherine Boucher in the Church of St Mary, Battersea	1794	*Songs of Innocence and of Experience*
			27 July: Execution of Robespierre
1783	*Poetical Sketches* printed		State Trials of British radical leaders
1784?	Writes *An Island in the Moon*		*Europe, a Prophecy*
1784–5	Partnership as print-seller with James Parker at 27 Broad Street		*The (First) Book of Urizen*
		1795	*The Song of Los*
			The Book of Ahania
1785	Moves to 28 Poland Street	*c.* 1795	The twelve large colour prints
1787	February: death of younger brother Robert	1795–7	Designs and engravings for Richard Edwards's edition of Young's *Night Thoughts*
c. 1788	*There is No Natural Religion, a* and *b*		
	All Religions are One	1797–	
1789	13 April: attends first General Conference of the New Jerusalem Church	1808?	*Vala or The Four Zoas* (unfinished)
		1798	Illustrations to the poems of Thomas Gray
	14 July: Fall of the Bastille		
	Songs of Innocence	1799	23 August: Blake's defence of his visionary art in a letter to Dr John Trusler, prompted by the latter's rejection of the watercolour *Malevolence*
c. 1789	*Tiriel*		
1789–93?	*The Book of Thel*		
1790	Edmund Burke: *Reflections on the Revolution in France*		9 November: Napoleon's *coup* of 18th Brumaire
	Autumn: moves to Hercules Buildings, Lambeth	1799–1800	Fifty tempera illustrations to the Bible for Thomas Butts
1790–3	*The Marriage of Heaven and Hell*	1800	18 September: moves to Felpham, Sussex. Association with William Hayley
1791	Thomas Paine: *The Rights of Man*		
	The French Revolution	1802	27 March: Peace of Amiens
1791–3	Engravings for *Narrative of a Five Years' Expedition Against the Revolted Negroes of Surinam* by John Gabriel Stedman		*Designs to a Series of Ballads* by William Hayley
		1803, 1804	William Hayley: *Life of William Cowper*, with six engravings by Blake
1792	23 February: death of Sir Joshua Reynolds		

1803	Seven watercolours for Butts on Biblical subjects 10 May: war against France resumes 12 August: Private John Scholfield is ejected by Blake from his garden and charges Blake with seditious utterances September: the Blakes return to London. Residence at 17 South Molton Street 4 October: At the Quarter Sessions at Petworth, Blake is indicted for sedition and assault
1804	11 January: Tried at Chichester, Blake is found not guilty October: the day after visiting the Truchsessian Gallery, Blake has an experience of illumination Title-pages of *Milton* and *Jerusalem* dated 1804, though neither work was ready for publication
1805	More watercolours for Butts on Biblical subjects October: Trafalgar; death of Nelson October: Commissioned by Robert Hartley Cromek, Blake illustrates Blair's *Grave*; also makes relief etching *Death's Door*
c. 1805–10	*Job* watercolours for Thomas Butts
1806	*Canterbury Pilgrims* controversy; breaks with Thomas Stothard *Last Judgment* for Thomas Butts
1807	January: more elaborate *Last Judgment* for Countess of Egremont Slave trade abolished
c. 1807	First *Paradise Lost* series
1808	Second *Paradise Lost* series August: *The Grave* published with twelve plates executed by L. Schiavonetti after Blake's designs
c. 1808	*Canterbury Pilgrims* tempera
1809	May: opens exhibition of his own work at the house of his brother James; paintings include the *Pitt* and the *Nelson*. Publishes *A Descriptive Catalogue*

	17 September: Robert Hunt attacks Blake in the *Examiner*
1809–10	First two copies of *Milton a Poem* produced
1810	An elaborate *Last Judgment* for Butts, and temperas including *Adam Naming the Beasts* and *Eve Naming the Birds* *Canterbury Pilgrims* engraving
1814	30 May: First Treaty of Paris
1815	18 June: Waterloo Copy D of *Milton* produced
c. 1815	Illustrations for *On the Morning of Christ's Nativity*
c. 1816	Illustrations for *L'Allegro* and *Il Penseroso*
1816–18	Illustrations for *Paradise Regained*
1818	June: meets John Linnell
c. 1818	*For the Sexes: The Gates of Paradise*
c. 1818	*Laocoön*
1819	16 August: Manchester Massacre October: begins drawing Visionary Heads for John Varley
1820?	*On Homers Poetry* and *On Virgil*
1819–1821	*Jerusalem* completed
1820	Wood engravings for Dr R. J. Thornton's *The Pastorals of Virgil*
1821	Moves to Fountain Court, Strand
1822	*The Ghost of Abel*
1823	Contracts with Linnell to engrave *Job* after his own designs
c. 1824	Illustrations to *Pilgrim's Progress* Linnell commissions Blake to illustrate Dante
1826	March: publication of *Illustrations of the Book of Job* Last copy of Jerusalem (F) produced
1826–7	Engraves seven Dante plates
1827	12 August: dies 17 August: buried in Bunhill Fields
1831	18 October: death of Catherine Blake

The Plates

For illuminated books, measurements are
given according to the design area, and for
engravings according to the platemark,
unless otherwise shown. Measurements are to
the nearest eighth of an inch.

Titles are given in Blake's own form
wherever possible. Where Blake's wording
is not known, titles have been standardized
according to modern usage.

1. *The Penance of Jane Shore in St Paul's Church*. About 1793. Pen and watercolour. $9\frac{5}{8} \times 11\frac{5}{8}$ in. London, Tate Gallery

2. *War* (*A Breach in a City*, later version). 1805. Watercolour. 11¾ × 15⅛ in. Cambridge, Massachusetts, Fogg Art Museum, Grenville L. Winthrop Bequest

3. *Tiriel: Har and Heva Bathing*. About 1785–9. Point of the brush, indian ink, grey wash. 7¼ × 10¾ in. Cambridge, Fitzwilliam Museum

4. *Edward & Elenor.* Inscribed 1793, but possibly about 1779–80. Line engraving. Platemark 14¾×20¼ in. London, British Museum

EZEKIEL.

I take away from thee the Desire of thine Eyes

5. *Ezekiel*. 1794. Line engraving. 18⅛ × 21¼ in. London, British Museum

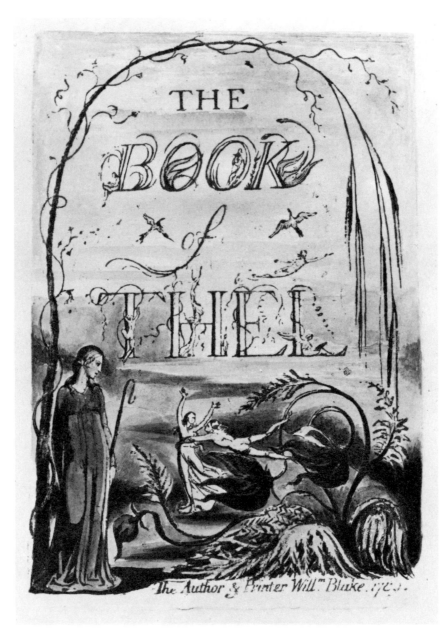

6. *The Book of Thel*, copy J, plate ii, title-page. 1789. Relief etching with water-
colour and watercolour washes. Page size $11\frac{5}{8} \times 9$ in; design area $5\frac{7}{8} \times 4\frac{1}{8}$ in.
Harvard University, Houghton Library

7. *Songs of Innocence and of Experience* (1793–4), copy B, plates 9 and 10, *The Little Black Boy*. Relief etching, colour-printed, with watercolour. $4\frac{1}{4} \times 2\frac{5}{8}$ in. London, British Museum

8. *The Marriage of Heaven and Hell*, copy F, plate 1, title-page.
1790–3. Relief etching, colour-printed, finished and
heightened with watercolour. 5¾×4 in. New York, Pierpont
Morgan Library (Thorne Collection)

9. *The Marriage of Heaven and Hell*, copy G, plate 11. 1790–3.
Relief etching with watercolour, strengthened in ink. 5⅞×4 in.
Harvard University, Houghton Library

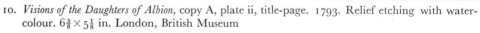

10. *Visions of the Daughters of Albion*, copy A, plate ii, title-page. 1793. Relief etching with water-colour. 6⅜ × 5⅛ in. London, British Museum

11. *Songs of Innocence and of Experience* (1789–94), copy I, plate 39, *The Sick Rose*. 1793. Relief etching with watercolour. 4⅜ × 2⅝ in. Harvard University, Houghton Library (Widener Collection)

12. *A Large Book of Designs*, 5: *Visions of the Daughters of Albion*, frontispiece. About 1795.
Colour-printed, finished with opaque pigments and watercolour. $6\frac{3}{4} \times 4\frac{3}{4}$ in. London,
British Museum

Preludium

The shadowy daughter of Urthona stood before red Orc.
When fourteen suns had faintly journeyd oer his dark abode;
His food she brought in iron baskets, his drink in cups of iron:
Crownd with a helmet & dark hair the nameless female stood;
A quiver with its burning stores, a bow like that of night,
When pestilence is shot from heaven; no other arms she need:
Invulnerable tho' naked, save where clouds roll round her loins,
Their awful folds in the dark air; silent she stood as night;
For never from her iron tongue could voice or sound arise;
But dumb till that dread day when Orc assayd his fierce embrace.

Dark virgin; said the hairy youth, thy father stern abhorrd;
Rivets my tenfold chains while still on high my spirit soars;
Sometimes an eagle screaming in the sky, sometimes a lion,
Stalking upon the mountains, & sometimes a whale I lash
The raging fathomless abyss, anon a serpent folding
Around the pillars of Urthona, and round thy dark limbs,
On the Canadian wilds I fold, feeble my spirit folds.
For chaind beneath I rend these caverns; when thou bringest food
I howl my joy: and my red eyes seek to behold thy face
In vain! these clouds roll to & fro, & hide thee from my sight.

13. *America*, copy F, plate 1. 1793. Relief etching, uncoloured. 9¾×6⅜ in. London, British Museum

Thus wept the Angel voice & as he wept the terrible blasts
Of trumpets, blew a loud alarm across the Atlantic deep.
No trumpets answer; no reply of clarions or of fifes,
Silent the Colonies remain and refuse the loud alarm.

On those vast shady hills between America & Albions shore;
Now barr'd out by the Atlantic sea: call'd Atlantean hills:
Because from their bright summits you may pass to the Golden world
An ancient palace, archetype of mighty Emperies.
Rears its immortal pinnacles, built in the forest of God
By Ariston the king of beauty for his stolen bride.

4 JY 59

Here on their magic seats the thirteen Angels sat perturb'd
For clouds from the Atlantic hover oer the solemn roof.

14. *America*, copy F, plate 10. 1793. Relief etching, uncoloured. 9¼×6⅝ in. London, British Museum

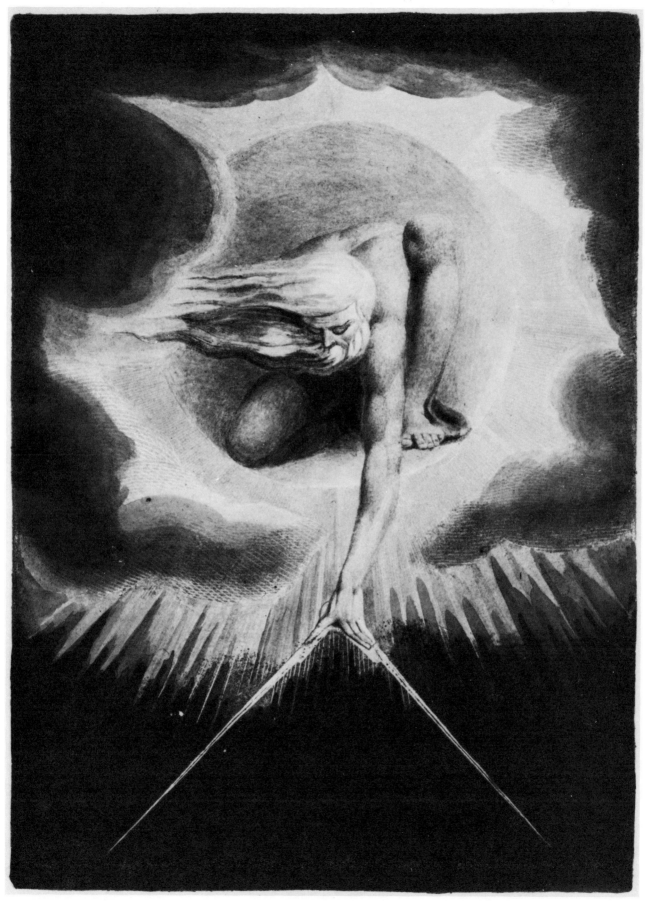

15. *Europe*, copy D, plate i, frontispiece. 1794. Relief etching, colour-printed, with watercolour washes. $9\frac{1}{4} \times 6\frac{5}{8}$ in. London, British Museum

16. *Europe*, copy D, plate 7. 1794. Relief etching, colour-printed, with watercolour washes. $9\frac{1}{4} \times 6\frac{5}{8}$ in. London, British Museum

Albions Angel rose upon the Stone of Night.
He saw Urizen on the Atlantic:
And his brazen Book,
That Kings & Priests had copied on Earth
Expanded from North to South.

17. *Europe*, copy H, plate 11. 1794. Relief etching, uncoloured, grey wash. 9½ × 7 in. Harvard University, Houghton Library

18. *The Song of Los*, copy D, plate 1, frontispiece. 1795. Relief etching, colour-printed, with opaque pigments. 9¼×6⅞ in. London, British Museum

In thunders ends the voice. Then Albions Angel wrathful burnt
Beside the Stone of Night; and like the eternal Lions howl
In famine & war, replyd. Art thou not Orc, who serpent-form'd
Stands at the gate of Enitharmon to devour her children;
Blasphemous Demon, Antichrist, hater of Dignities;
Lover of wild rebellion, and transgresser of Gods Law;
Why dost thou come to Angels eyes in this terrific form?

19. *America*, copy O, plate 7. 1793. Relief etching, painted with watercolours and gold. 9¼ × 6½ in. Cambridge, Fitzwilliam Museum

20. *The Song of Los*, copy A, plate 5. 1795. Relief etching, colour-printed, with opaque pigments. $9\frac{1}{8} \times 6\frac{3}{8}$ in. London,
British Museum

21. *Oberon and Titania*. About 1793. Watercolour. $8\frac{3}{8} \times 6\frac{1}{2}$ in. Private Collection

22. *The First Book of Urizen*, copy D, plate 11. 1794. Relief etching, colour-printed, with opaque pigments. 5¾ × 4⅛ in. London, British Museum

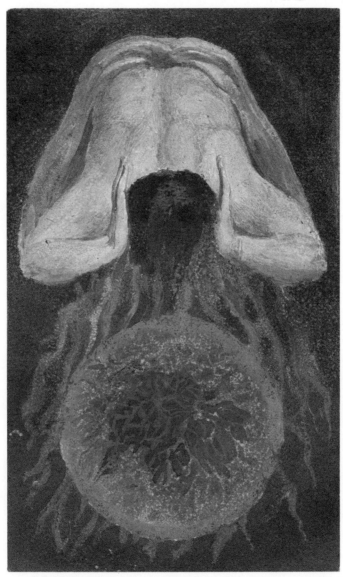

23. *A Small Book of Designs, 3: The Book of Urizen*, plate 17. 1795–6.
Relief etching, colour-printed. $5\frac{3}{4} \times 3\frac{5}{8}$ in. London, British
Museum

25. *The Book of Ahania*, copy A, plate 1, frontispiece. 1795. Intaglio etching, colour-printed in blue and grey. $5\frac{1}{4} \times 3\frac{7}{8}$ in. Washington, Library of Congress, Lessing J. Rosenwald Collection

24. *The First Book of Urizen*, copy D, plate 21. 1794. Relief etching, some colour-printing, mostly coloured with watercolour. $6\frac{1}{2} \times 4$ in. London, British Museum

26. *Hecate.* 1795. Colour-printed monotype, finished with pen and watercolour. $17\frac{1}{4} \times 22\frac{7}{8}$ in. London, Tate Gallery

27. *A Large Book of Designs, 2: Our End is come.* 1794–5. Line engraving, colour-printed.
$8\frac{1}{2} \times 4\frac{3}{4}$ in. London, British Museum

28. *Elohim Creating Adam.* 1795. Colour-printed monotype, finished with pen and watercolour. $17 \times 21\frac{1}{8}$ in. London, Tate Gallery

29. *Nebuchadnezzar*. 1795. Colour-printed monotype, finished with pen and watercolour. $16\frac{3}{4} \times 23\frac{3}{4}$ in. Minneapolis Institute of Arts

30. *Newton*. 1795. Colour-printed monotype, finished with pen and watercolour. $17\frac{3}{8} \times 22\frac{1}{4}$ in. London, Tate Gallery

31. *The Good and Evil Angels.* 1795. Colour-printed monotype, finished with pen and watercolour. $17\frac{1}{2} \times 23\frac{3}{8}$ in. London, Tate Gallery

32. *God Writing Upon the Tables of the Covenant*. About 1805. Watercolour. 16½ × 13½ in. Edinburgh, National Gallery of Scotland

33. *The House of Death*. 1795. Colour-printed monotype, finished with watercolour. $18\frac{7}{8} \times 23\frac{7}{8}$ in. London, Tate Gallery

34. *Lucifer and the Pope in Hell*. About 1795 or earlier. Colour-printed line engraving. 7¼ × 9¾ in. San Marino, California, Henry E. Huntington Library and Art Gallery

THE

COMPLAINT.

OR,

𝕹ight-𝕿houghts

ON

LIFE, DEATH, and IMMORTALITY.

NIGHT *the* EIGHTH.

VIRTUE's APOLOGY:

OR,

The MAN *of the* WORLD *Answer'd.*

In which are Confidered,

The LOVE *of* THIS LIFE;

The AMBITION *and* PLEASURE, *with the* WIT
and WISDOM *of the* WORLD.

LONDON:

Printed for G. HAWKINS, at *Milton's* Head, between the *Two Temple-
Gates, Fleet-street,* near *Temple-Bar.*
And Sold by M. COOPER, at the *Globe,* in *Pater-noster Row.*

MDCCXLV.

35. Young's *Night Thoughts*, Night VIII, title-page. 1795–6. Watercolour. 20½ × 15¾ in. London, British Museum

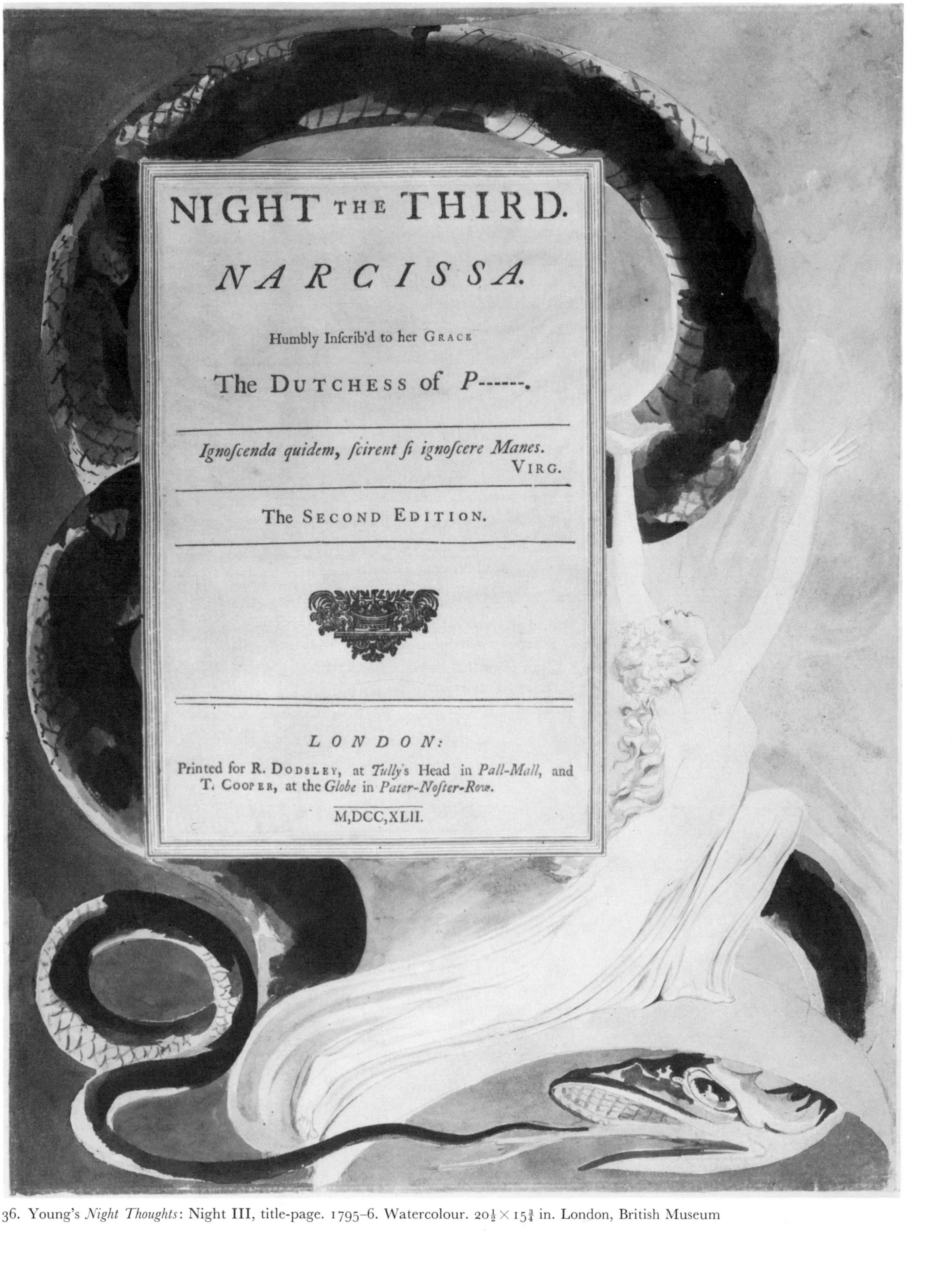
NIGHT THE THIRD.
NARCISSA.
Humbly Inſcrib'd to her GRACE
The DUTCHESS of P------.
Ignoſcenda quidem, ſcirent ſi ignoſcere Manes.
VIRG.
The SECOND EDITION.
LONDON:
Printed for R. DODSLEY, at Tully's Head in Pall-Mall, and
T. COOPER, at the Globe in Pater-Noſter-Row.
M,DCC,XLII.

36. Young's *Night Thoughts*: Night III, title-page. 1795–6. Watercolour. $20\frac{1}{2} \times 15\frac{3}{4}$ in. London, British Museum

But rises in demand for her delay;
She makes a scourge of past prosperity
To sting thee more, and double thy distress.

 LORENZO, fortune makes her court to thee;
Thy fond heart dances, while the syren sings:
Dear is thy welfare; think me not unkind,
I would not damp, but to secure thy joys:
Think not that fear is sacred to the storm;
Stand on thy guard against the smiles of fate.
Is heaven tremendous in its frowns? most sure—
And in its favours formidable too:
* Its favours here are trials, not rewards;
A call to duty, not discharge from care;
And should alarm us, full as much as woes;
Awake us to their cause and consequence;
And make us tremble, weigh'd with our desert.
Awe nature's tumults, and chastise her joys,
Lest, while we clasp, we kill them; nay, invert
To worse than simple misery their charms:
Revolted joys, like foes in civil war,
Like bosom friendships to resentment sour'd,
With rage envenom'd rise against our peace.
Beware what earth calls happiness; beware
All joys, but joys that never can expire:
Who builds on less than an immortal base,
Fond as he seems, condemns his joys to death.

 Mine died with thee, PHILANDER! thy last sigh
Dissolved the charm; the disenchanted earth
Lost all her lustre: where her glitt'ring towers?
Her golden mountains where?—all darken'd down

37. Young's *Night Thoughts*, p. 12. 1797. Intaglio engraving. 14⅞ × 12⅜ in. London, British Museum

23

Pregnant with all eternity can give ;
Pregnant with all that makes archangels smile :
Who murders time, he crushes in the birth
A power ethereal, only not adored.

    Ah ! how unjust to nature and himself,
Is thoughtless, thankless, inconsistent man !
Like children babbling nonsense in their sports,
* We censure nature for a span too short ;
That span too short, we tax as tedious too ;
Torture invention, all expedients tire,
To lash the ling'ring moments into speed,
And whirl us, happy riddance ! from ourselves.
Art, brainless art ! our furious charioteer,
For nature's voice unstifled would recall,
Drives headlong tow'rds the precipice of death—
Death, most our dread ; death thus more dreadful made
O what a riddle of absurdity !
Leisure is pain ; take off our chariot-wheels,
How heavily we drag the load of life !
Blest leisure is our curse ; like that of Cain,
It makes us wander ; wander earth around
To fly that tyrant, thought.   As Atlas groan'd
The world beneath, we groan beneath an hour :
We cry for mercy to the next amusement ;
The next amusement mortgages our fields—
Slight inconvenience ! prisons hardly frown—
From hateful time if prisons set us free ;
Yet when death kindly tenders us relief,
We call him cruel ; years to moments shrink,
Ages to years : the telescope is turn'd,

38. Young's *Night Thoughts*, p. 23. 1797. Intaglio engraving. 14¼ × 11⅛ in. Oxford, Ashmolean Museum

35

Had thought been all, sweet speech had been denied;
Speech, thought's canal! speech, thought's criterion too!
Thought in the mine may come forth gold or dross;
When coin'd in words, we know its real worth:
If sterling, store it for thy future use;
'Twill buy thee benefit, perhaps renown:
Thought too, deliver'd, is the more possess'd;
* Teaching, we learn; and giving, we retain
The births of intellect; when dumb, forgot.
Speech ventilates our intellectual fire;
Speech burnishes our mental magazine;
Brightens for ornament, and whets for use.
What numbers, sheath'd in erudition, lie
Plunged to the hilts in venerable tomes,
And rusted; who might have borne an edge,
And play'd a sprightly beam, if born to speech!
If born blest heirs to half their mother's tongue!
'Tis thought's exchange, which, like th' alternate push
Of waves conflicting, breaks the learned scum,
And defecates the student's standing pool.
    In contemplation is his proud resource?
'Tis poor as proud: by converse unsustain'd
Rude thought runs wild in contemplation's field:
Converse, the menage, breaks it to the bit
Of due restraint; and emulation's spur
Gives graceful energy, by rivals awed:
'Tis converse qualifies for solitude,
As exercise for salutary rest:
By that untutor'd, contemplation raves;
And nature's fool, by wisdom's is outdone.

39. Young's *Night Thoughts*, p. 35. 1797. Intaglio engraving. $15\frac{1}{8} \times 12\frac{5}{8}$ in. Oxford, Ashmolean Museum

40. Gray's *Poems*: no. 11, *Ode on the Death of a Favourite Cat (Drowned in a Tub of Gold Fishes)*. 1798. Watercolour. 16⅜ × 12½ in. Yale Center for British Art, Mr and Mrs Paul Mellon Collection

41. *Malevolence*. 1799. Pen and watercolour. $11\frac{7}{8} \times 8\frac{7}{8}$ in. Philadelphia Museum of Art

42. *Vala or The Four Zoas*, p. 86. 1797–1807. Pencil and crayon. Page size 16⅛ × 12⅝ in. London, British Museum

Albion rose from where he labourd at the Mill with Slaves
Giving himself for the Nations he danc'd the dance of Eternal Death

43. *Albion rose* (*'Glad Day'*). 1800–3. Line engraving. Platemark 10⅝ × 7¾ in. Washington, National Gallery of Art, Lessing J. Rosenwald Collection

Inside the design, hand-lettered:

A Series of Designs:
Illustrative of
The Grave.
a Poem
by Robert Blair.

Invented & Drawn by William Blake
1806

44. *Design for an Album*: Title-page for Blair's *Grave*. 1806. Watercolour. 9⅜ × 7⅞ in. San Marino, California, Henry E. Huntington Library and Art Gallery

45. Blair's *Grave: Death's Door*. About 1806–7. Relief etching, white line.
$6\frac{1}{4} \times 4\frac{1}{2}$ in. Lucile Rosenbloom Collection

Drawn by W. Blake   Etched by L. Schiavonetti

46. Blair's *Grave: Death's Door*.
Engraving by Lewis Schiavonetti after Blake. 1808. 9½ × 5¼
in. London, Victoria and
Albert Museum

47. *The spiritual form of Nelson guiding Leviathan.* About 1806–9. Tempera on canvas. 30×24⅝ in. London, Tate Gallery

48. *The spiritual form of Pitt, guiding Behemoth.* 1806–9. Tempera heightened with gold on canvas. 29⅛ × 24¾ in. London, Tate Gallery

49. *The Fall of Man.* 1807. Watercolour. 19¼ × 15⅛ in. London, Victoria and Albert Museum

50. *The Last Judgment.* 1808. Watercolour and pen over pencil. 19⅞ × 15¾ in. Petworth House, Sussex, The National Trust

51. *The Bard*, from Gray (recto). 1809. Pencil. 25½ × 18½ in. Philadelphia Museum of Art, Louise and Walter Arensberg Collection

52. *Milton*, copy B, plate 18 (*Census* 15). 1804–9. Relief etching, painted in
watercolour. 6¾ × 4¼ in. San Marino, California, Henry E. Huntington
Library and Art Gallery

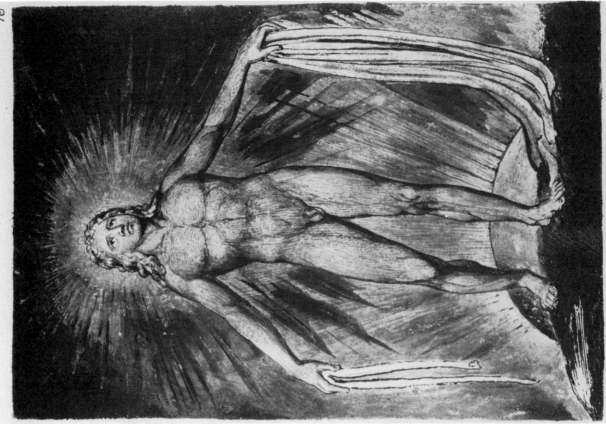

16

54. *Milton*, copy D, plate 16 (*Census* 13). 1804–15. Relief etching, painted in watercolour and some gold. 6¼×4¼ in. Washington, Library of Congress, Lessing J. Rosenwald Collection

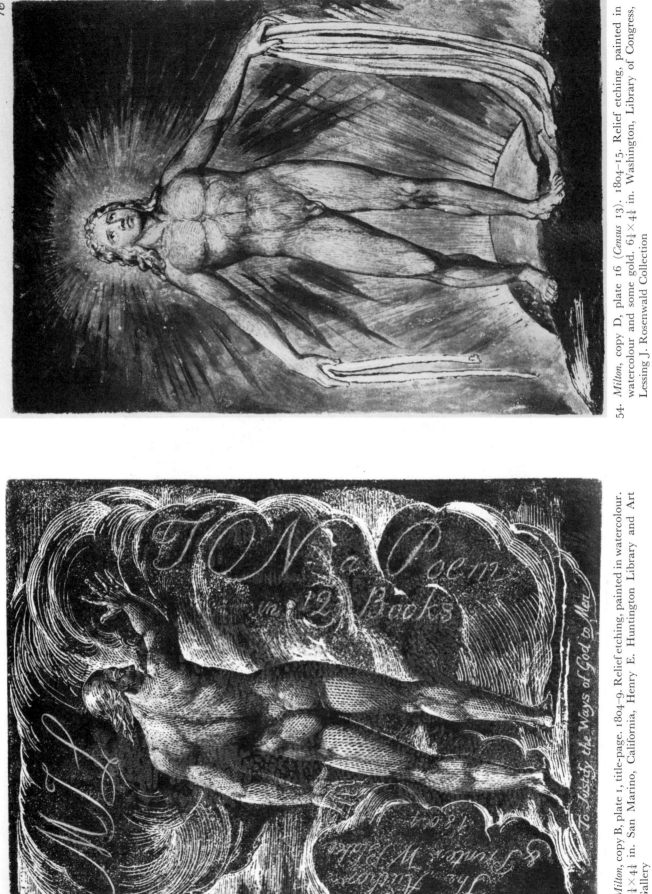

53. *Milton*, copy B, plate 1, title-page. 1804–9. Relief etching, painted in watercolour. 6¼×4¼ in. San Marino, California, Henry E. Huntington Library and Art Gallery

56. *Milton*, copy B, plate 42 (*Census* 38). 1804–9. Relief etching, painted in watercolour. 6¼ × 4½ in. San Marino, California, Henry E. Huntington Library and Art Gallery

55. *Milton*, copy D, plate 37 (*Census* 33). 1804–15. Relief etching, outlined in ink, painted in watercolour, opaque pigments and gold. 6⅝ × 4¾ in. Washington, Library of Congress, Lessing J. Rosenwald Collection

57. Milton's *Il Penseroso: Milton and the Spirit of Plato*. About 1816. Watercolour. $6\frac{3}{8} \times 4\frac{7}{8}$ in.
New York, Pierpont Morgan Library

58. Milton's *Il Penseroso: Milton in his Old Age*. About 1816. Watercolour. $6\frac{1}{4} \times 4\frac{7}{8}$ in. New York, Pierpont Morgan Library

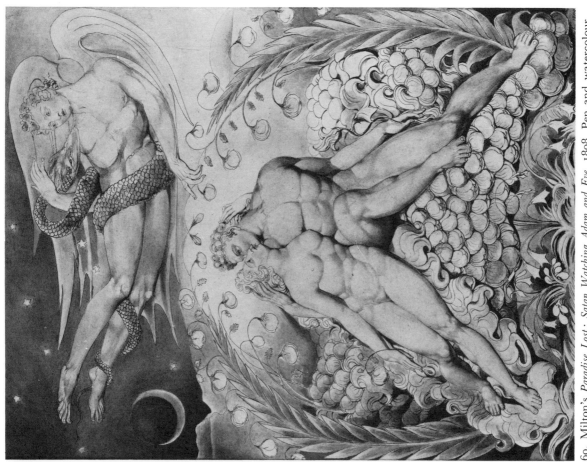

60. Milton's *Paradise Lost: Satan Watching Adam and Eve.* 1808. Pen and watercolour. 20 × 15¼ in. Boston, Museum of Fine Arts

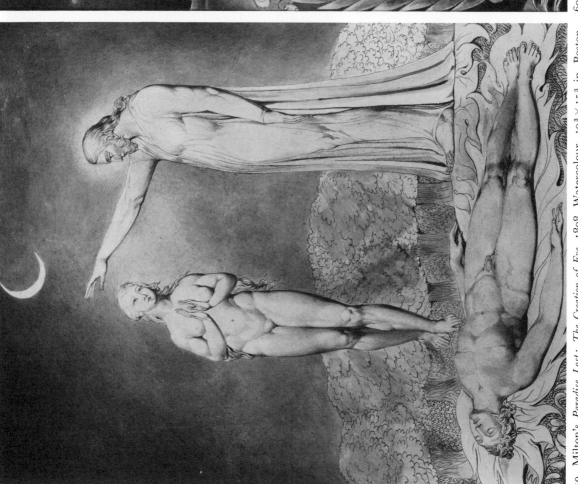

59. Milton's *Paradise Lost: The Creation of Eve.* 1808. Watercolour. 19¾ × 15¾ in. Boston, Museum of Fine Arts

62. Milton's *Paradise Regained: Christ Tempted by Satan to Turn the Stones Into Bread*. About 1816–18. Watercolour with indian ink and grey wash. 6⅞ × 5¼ in. Cambridge, Fitzwilliam Museum

61. *Mirth and her Companions*. About 1816–20. Line and stipple engraving, second state. 6¾ × 5⅞ in. Sir Geoffrey Keynes Collection

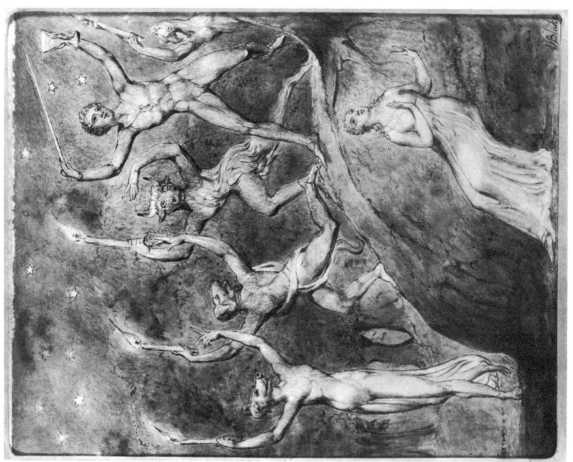

64. Milton's *Comus*: *Comus with His Revellers*. About 1810–15. Pen and watercolour. 6 × 4¾ in. Boston, Museum of Fine Arts

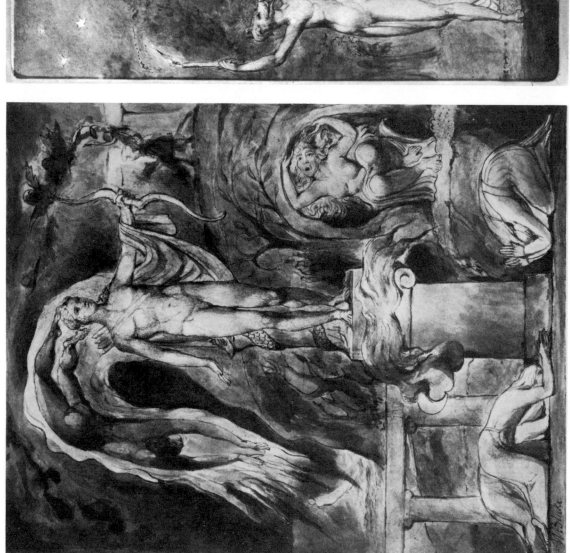

63. Milton's *Hymn on the Morning of Christ's Nativity*: *The Overthrow of Apollo and the Pagan Gods*. About 1815–16. Watercolour. 6¼ × 4⅞ in. San Marino, California, Henry E. Huntington Library and Art Gallery

66. *A Spirit vaulting from a cloud.* 1809. Pen, ink and watercolour. 9¼ × 6¾ in. London, British Museum

65. *Satan calling up his Legions.* Not dated. Tempera on canvas. 21¼ × 16½ in. London, Victoria and Albert Museum

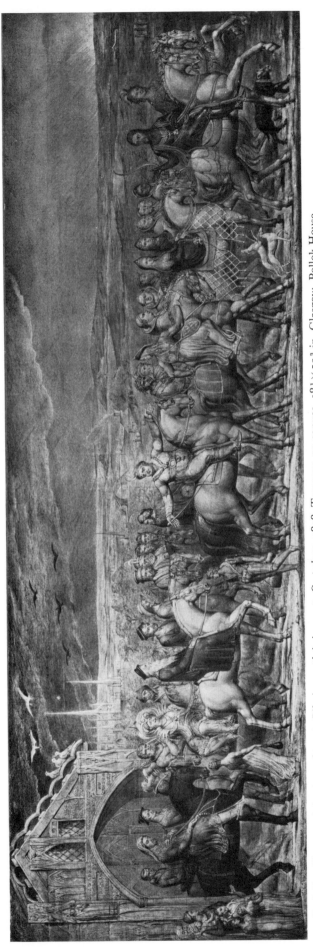

67. *Sir Jeffrey Chaucer and the nine and twenty Pilgrims on their journey to Canterbury*. 1808. Tempera on canvas. 18¼ × 53¾ in. Glasgow, Pollok House

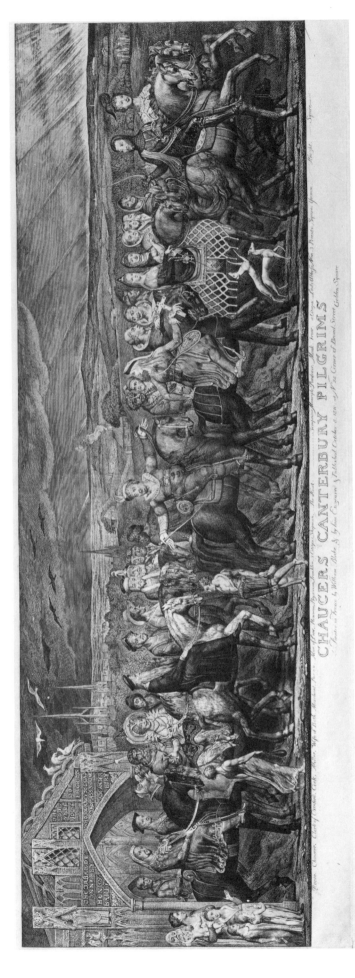

68. *Chaucers Canterbury Pilgrims*. About 1810–11. Line engraving, second state. Platemark 13⅞ × 38 in. London, British Museum

69. *Heads of the Poets: John Milton.* About 1800–3. Tempera on canvas. 15¾ × 35¼ in. Manchester City Art Gallery

70. *Heads of the Poets: Edmund Spenser.* 1800–3. Tempera on canvas. 16½ × 33 in. Manchester City Art Gallery

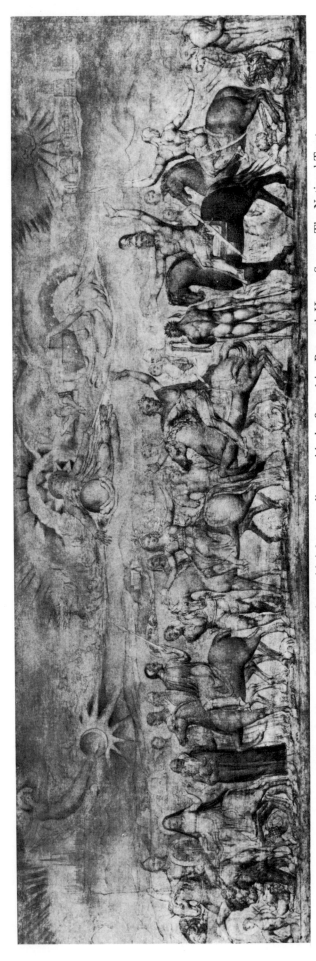

71. *The Characters in Spenser's 'Faerie Queene'*. About 1825. Watercolour with ink on muslin, varnished. 18 × 53½ in. Petworth House, Sussex, The National Trust

72. *The Characters in Spenser's 'Faerie Queene'* (detail of *Pl.* 71)

73. *Moses Erecting the Brazen Serpent.* About 1805. Pen and watercolour. 13⅜ × 12¾ in. Boston, Museum of Fine Arts

74. *The Pardon of Absalom.* About 1800–5. Watercolour. 12½ × 14¾ in. Bedford, Cecil Higgins Art Gallery

75. *The Baptism of Christ.* 1799–1800. Tempera on canvas. 12¾ × 19⅜ in. Rhode Island School of Design, Museum of Art

76. *The Circumcision.* 1799–1800. Tempera on canvas. 10 × 14½ in. Sir Geoffrey Keynes Collection

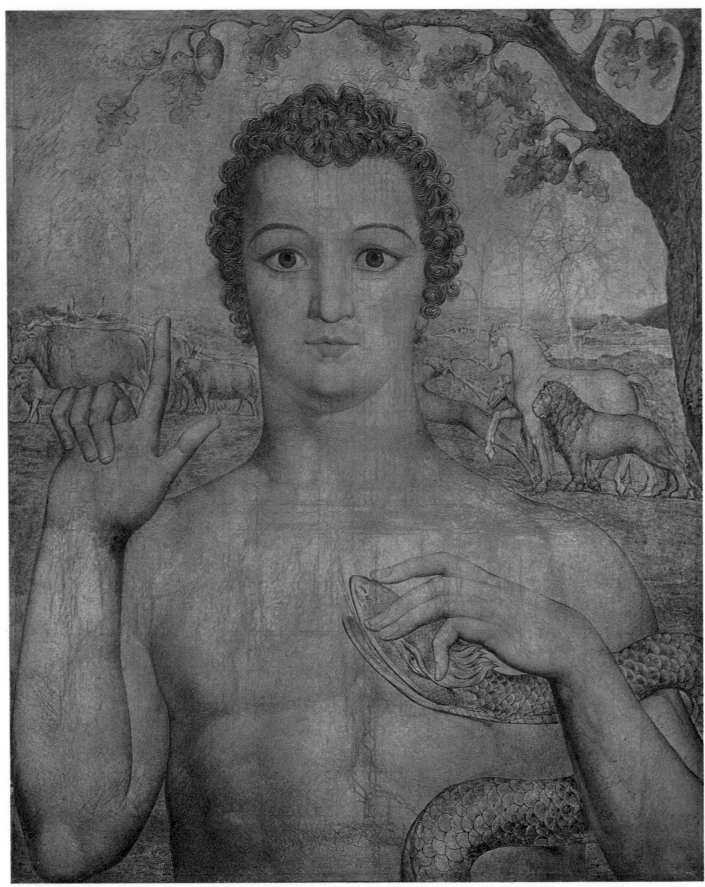

77. *Adam naming the Beasts.* 1810. Tempera on canvas. 29½ × 24½ in. Glasgow, Pollok House

78. *The Virgin and Child in Egypt*. 1810. Tempera on canvas. 28¾ × 23¾ in. London, Victoria and Albert Museum

79. *Christ's Entry into Jerusalem*. 1800. Oil on copper. 12¼ × 18⅞ in. Glasgow, Pollok House

80. *The Last Supper*. 1799–1800. Tempera on canvas. 9 × 12 in. Washington, National Gallery of Art, Lessing J. Rosenwald Collection

81. *The Woman Taken in Adultery.* About 1805. Watercolour over traces of pencil. 14 × 14⅛ in. Boston, Museum of Fine Arts

82. *The Four and Twenty Elders Casting Their Crowns Before the Divine Throne.* 1805. Pencil and watercolour. 14 × 11½ in. London, Tate Gallery

83. *Mary Magdalen at the Sepulchre.* About 1805. Pen and indian ink with some watercolour. 16¾ × 12 in. Yale Center for British Art, Mr and Mrs Paul Mellon Collection

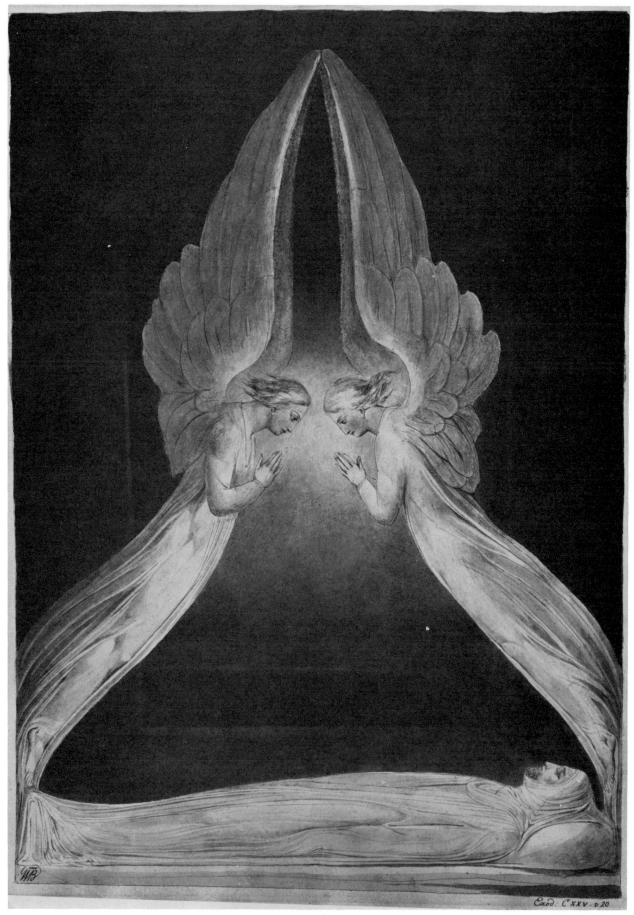

84. *The Angels hovering over the Body of Jesus in the Sepulchre.* About 1805. Pen and ink and watercolour. $16\frac{1}{4} \times 11\frac{7}{8}$ in. London, Victoria and Albert Museum

85. *The Great Red Dragon and the Woman Clothed with the Sun*. About 1805. Watercolour. 17½ × 13½ in. The Brooklyn Museum

86. *Theotormon Woven.* About 1806–20.
Pencil. $4\frac{3}{8} \times 3$ in. London, Victoria and
Albert Museum

87. *The Head of the Ghost of a Flea.*
1819. Pencil. $7\frac{1}{2} \times 6$ in. London,
Tate Gallery

88. *Epitome of James Hervey's 'Meditations among the Tombs'*. 1820–4. Pen and watercolour. $16\frac{7}{8} \times 11\frac{1}{2}$ in. London, Tate Gallery

89. '*The Arlington Court Picture*'. 1821. Watercolour on prepared ground of thin gesso. $16 \times 19\frac{1}{2}$ in. Arlington Court, Devon, The National Trust

90. *The Judgment of Paris*. 1811. Watercolour. $15\frac{1}{2} \times 18\frac{1}{2}$ in. London, British Museum

91. *Genesis* MS., second title-page. 1821 or later. Pencil with touches of watercolour. 14⅞ × 10¾ in. San Marino, California, Henry E. Huntington Library and Art Gallery

92. *The Man Sweeping the Interpreter's Parlour.* 1821–2. Engraving on pewter, second state. $3\frac{1}{8} \times 6\frac{1}{4}$ in. London, British Museum

93. Bunyan's *The Pilgrim's Progress: Christian beaten down by Apollyon.* 1824. Watercolour. $7\frac{1}{2} \times 5$ in. New York, Frick Collection

Engraved by W Blake 1773 from an old Italian Drawing
This is One of the Gothic Artists who Built the Cathedrals in what we call the Dark Ages
Wandering about in sheep skins & goat skins of whom the World was not worthy
                                                                    such were the Christians
Michael Angelo Pinxit.   in all Ages

94. *Joseph of Arimathea among The Rocks of Albion*. About 1809–20. Line engraving, second state. Platemark $10\frac{1}{8} \times 5\frac{1}{2}$ in. London, British Museum

95. *Laocoön.* About 1818. Line engraving. Engraved surface 10⅜×8⅝ in. Platemark 10¾×9 in. Sir Geoffrey Keynes Collection

96. *Jerusalem*, plate 1, frontispiece (proof). 1804–20. Relief etching printed in black and brown; lettering picked out in black. 8¾ × 6⅜ in. Sir Geoffrey Keynes Collection

97. *Jerusalem*, copy A, plate 2, title-page. 1804–20. Relief etching. 8¾×6¼ in. London, British Museum

Then the Divine hand found the Two Limits, Satan and Adam,
In Albions bosom: for in every Human bosom those Limits stand.
And the Divine voice came from the Furnaces, as multitudes without
Number! the voices of the innumerable multitudes of Eternity.
And the appearance of a Man was seen in the Furnaces;
Saving those who have sinned from the punishment of the Law,
In pity of the punisher whose state is eternal death,
And keeping them from Sin by the mild counsels of his love.

Albion goes to Eternal Death: In Me all Eternity.
Must pass thro' condemnation, and awake beyond the Grave!
No individual can keep these Laws, for they are death
To every energy of man, and forbid the springs of life.
Albion hath enterd the State Satan! Be permanent O State!
And be thou for ever accursed! that Albion may arise again:
And be thou created into a State! I go forth to Create
States: to deliver Individuals evermore! Amen.

So spoke the voice from the Furnaces, descending into Non-Entity

98. *Jerusalem*, copy A, plate 31 (*Census* 35). 1804–20. Relief etching. 8¾ × 6¼ in. London, British Museum

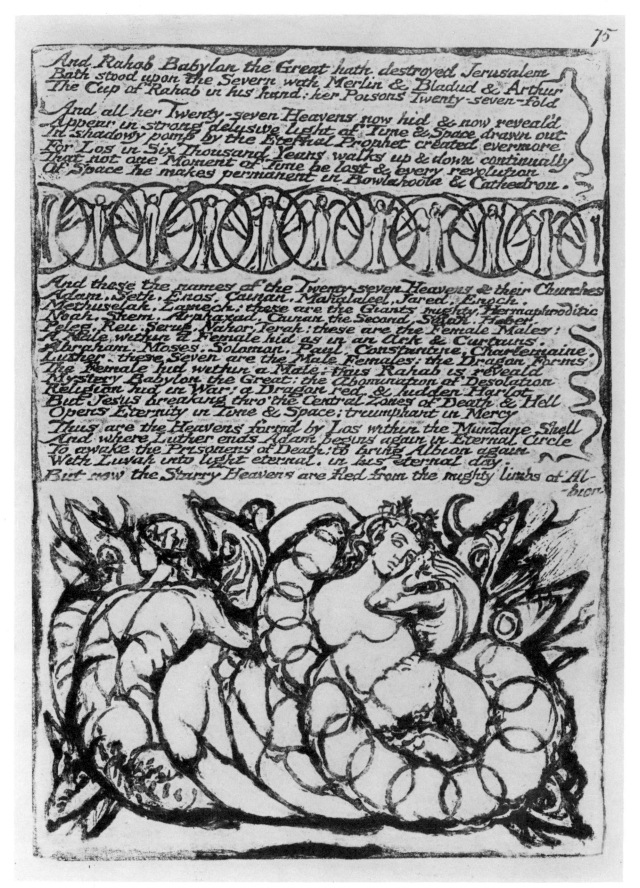

And Rahab Babylon the Great hath destroyed Jerusalem
Bath stood upon the Severn with Merlin & Bladud & Arthur
The Cup of Rahab in his hand: her Poisons Twenty-seven-fold

And all her Twenty-seven Heavens now hid & now reveald
Appear in strong delusive light of Time & Space drawn out
In shadowy pomp by the Eternal Prophet created evermore
For Los in Six Thousand Years walks up & down continually
That not one Moment of Time be lost & every revolution
Of Space he makes permanent in Bowlahoola & Cathedron.

And these the names of the Twenty-seven Heavens & their Churches
Adam. Seth. Enos. Cainan. Mahalaleel. Jared. Enoch.
Methuselah. Lamech: these are the Giants mighty Hermaphroditic
Noah. Shem. Arphaxad. Cainan the Second. Salah. Heber.
Peleg. Reu. Serug. Nahor. Terah: these are the Female Males:
A Male within a Female hid as in an Ark & Curtains.
Abraham. Moses. Solomon. Paul. Constantine. Charlemaine.
Luther. these Seven are the Male Females: the Dragon Forms
The Female hid within a Male: thus Rahab is reveald
Mystery Babylon the Great: the Abomination of Desolation
Religion hid in War: a Dragon red, & hidden Harlot
But Jesus breaking thro' the Central Zones of Death & Hell
Opens Eternity in Time & Space: triumphant in Mercy
Thus are the Heavens formd by Los within the Mundane Shell
And where Luther ends Adam begins again in Eternal Circle
To awake the Prisoners of Death: to bring Albion again
With Luvah into light eternal, in his eternal day.
But now the Starry Heavens are fled from the mighty limbs of Al-
-bion

99. *Jerusalem*, copy F, plate 75. 1820–6. Relief etching. 8 × 6¼ in. New York, Pierpont Morgan Library

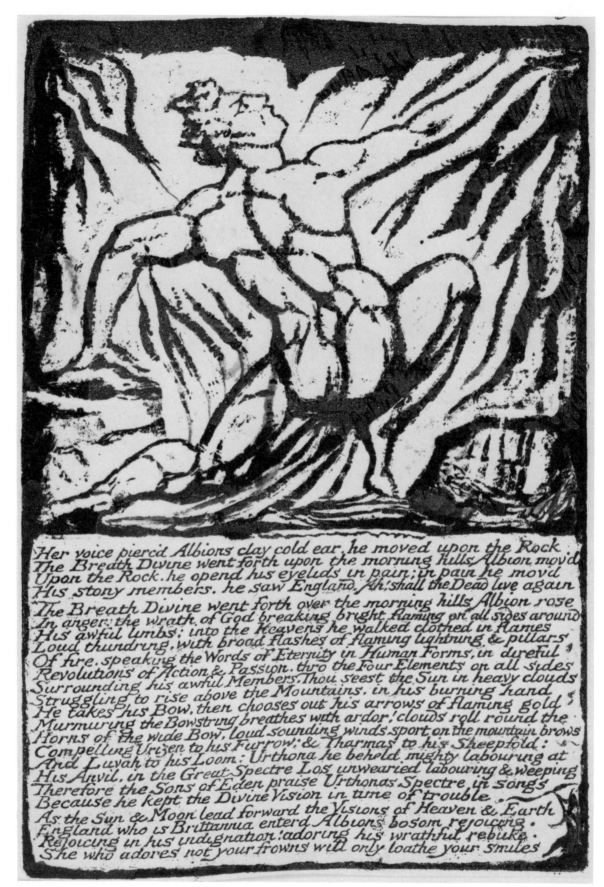

Her voice pierc'd Albions clay cold ear. he moved upon the Rock.
The Breath Divine went forth upon the morning hills, Albion mov'd
Upon the Rock. he opend his eyelids in pain; in pain he mov'd
His stony members. he saw England. Ah! shall the Dead live again

The Breath Divine went forth over the morning hills Albion rose
In anger: the wrath of God breaking bright flaming on all sides around
His awful limbs: into the Heavens he walked clothed in flames
Loud thundring, with broad flashes of flaming lightning & pillars
Of fire. speaking the Words of Eternity in Human Forms, in direful
Revolutions of Action & Passion. thro the Four Elements on all sides
Surrounding his awful Members. Thou seest the Sun in heavy clouds
Struggling to rise above the Mountains. in his burning hand
He takes his Bow, then chooses out his arrows of flaming gold
Murmuring the Bowstring breathes with ardor! clouds roll round the
Horns of the wide Bow, loud sounding winds sport on the mountain brows
Compelling Urizen to his Furrow: & Tharmas to his Sheepfold:
And Luvah to his Loom: Urthona he beheld mighty labouring at
His Anvil, in the Great Spectre Los unwearied labouring & weeping
Therefore the Sons of Eden praise Urthonas Spectre in songs
Because he kept the Divine Vision in time of trouble.

As the Sun & Moon lead forward the Visions of Heaven & Earth
England who is Brittannia enterd Albions bosom rejoicing.
Rejoicing in his indignation! adoring his wrathful rebuke.
She who adores not your frowns will only loathe your smiles

100. *Jerusalem*, copy A, plate 95. 1804–20. Relief etching. $8\frac{7}{8} \times 5\frac{3}{8}$ in. London, British Museum

101. *Jerusalem*, copy E, plate 100. 1804–20. Relief etching coloured with watercolour and gold. 8¾ × 5¾ in. Yale Center for British Art, Mr and Mrs Paul Mellon Collection

Jerusalem.
Chap: 2.

Every ornament of perfection. and every labour of love,
In all the Garden of Eden. & in all the golden mountains
Was become an envied horror. and a remembrance of jealousy:
And every Act a Crime. and Albion the punisher & judge.

And Albion spoke from his secret seat and said

All these ornaments are crimes, they are made by the labours
Of loves: of unnatural consanguinities and friendships
Horrid to think of when enquired deeply into; and all
These hills & valleys are accursed witnesses of Sin
I therefore. condense them into solid rocks. stedfast:
A foundation and certainty and demonstrative truth:
That Man be separate from Man, & here I plant my seat.

Cold snows drifted around him: ice coverd his loins around
He sat by Tyburns brook. and underneath his heel. shot up:
A deadly Tree. he nam'd it Moral Virtue. and the Law
Of God who dwells in Chaos hidden from the human sight.

The Tree spread over him its cold shadows. (Albion groand)
They bent down. they felt the earth and again enrooting
Shot into many a Tree! an endless labyrinth of woe!

From willing sacrifice of Self. to sacrifice of (miscall'd) Enemies
For Atonement: Albion began to erect twelve Altars,
Of rough unhewn rocks. before the Potters Furnace
He nam'd them Justice. and Truth. And Albions Sons
Must have become the first Victims. being the first transgressons
But they fled to the mountains to seek ransom: building A Strong
Fortification against the Divine Humanity. and Mercy.
In Shame & Jealousy to annihilate Jerusalem.

102. *Jerusalem*, plate 28 (trial proof). 1804–20. Relief etching. 8¾ × 6¼ in. New York, Pierpont Morgan Library

Jerusalem.
Chap: 2.

Every ornament of perfection, and every labour of love,
In all the Garden of Eden, & in all the golden mountains
Was become an envied horror, and a remembrance of jealousy:
And every Act a Crime, and Albion the punisher & judge.

And Albion spoke from his secret seat and said

All these ornaments are crimes, they are made by the labours
Of loves: of unnatural consanguinities and friendships
Horrid to think of when enquired deeply into; and all
These hills & valleys are accursed witnesses of Sin
I therefore condense them into solid rocks, stedfast!
A foundation and certainty and demonstrative truth:
That Man be separate from Man, & here I plant my seat.

Cold snows drifted around him: ice coverd his loins around
He sat by Tyburns brook, and underneath his heel, shot up!
A deadly Tree, he namd it Moral Virtue, and the Law
Of God who dwells in Chaos hidden from the human sight.

The Tree spread over him its cold shadows, (Albion groand)
They bent down, they felt the earth and again enrooting
Shot into many a Tree! an endless labyrinth of woe!

From willing sacrifice of Self, to sacrifice of (miscall'd) Enemies
For Atonement: Albion began to erect twelve Altars,
Of rough unhewn rocks, before the Potters Furnace
He namd them Justice, and Truth. And Albions Sons
Must have become the first Victims, being the first transgressors
But they fled to the mountains to seek ransom: building A Strong
Fortification against the Divine Humanity and Mercy,
In Shame & Jealousy to annihilate Jerusalem

103. *Jerusalem*, copy E, plate 28. 1804–20. Relief etching coloured with watercolour and gold. 8¾ × 6¼ in. Yale Center for British Art, Mr and Mrs Paul Mellon Collection

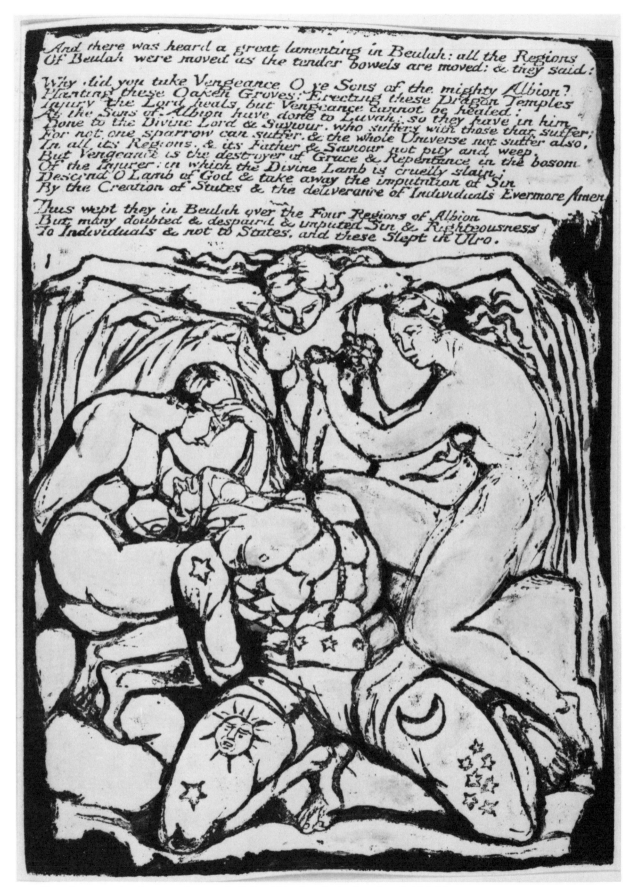

And there was heard a great lamenting in Beulah: all the Regions
Of Beulah were moved as the tender bowels are moved: & they said:

Why did you take Vengeance O ye Sons of the mighty Albion?
Planting these Oaken Groves: Erecting these Dragon Temples
Injury the Lord heals but Vengeance cannot be healed:
As the Sons of Albion have done to Luvah: so they have in him
Done to the Divine Lord & Saviour. who suffers with those that suffer;
For not one sparrow can suffer, & the whole Universe not suffer also,
In all its Regions, & its Father & Saviour not pity and weep.
But Vengeance is the destroyer of Grace & Repentance in the bosom
Of the Injurer: in which the Divine Lamb is cruelly slain:
Descend O Lamb of God & take away the imputation of Sin
By the Creation of States & the deliverance of Individuals Evermore Amen

Thus wept they in Beulah over the Four Regions of Albion
But many doubted & despaird & imputed Sin & Righteousness
To Individuals & not to States, and these Slept in Uro.

104. *Jerusalem*, copy A, plate 25. 1804–20. Relief etching. 8¾ × 6¼ in. London, British Museum

105. Study for *Jerusalem*, plate 25. Red crayon on ivory paper. 6½ × 9 in. Cambridge, Massachusetts, Fogg Art Museum

106. Study for *Jerusalem*, plate 51. Pencil. 6¼ × 13⅜ in. Hamburg, Kunsthalle

107. *Jerusalem*, copy E, plate 51. 1804–20. Relief etching coloured with watercolour and gold. $6\frac{1}{4} \times 8\frac{3}{4}$ in. Yale Center for British Art, Mr and Mrs Paul Mellon Collection

108. *The Book of Job: Behold now Behemoth which I made with thee.* About 1805–10. Pen, ink wash and watercolour. 10¾ × 7¾ in. New York, Pierpont Morgan Library

109. *Job and his Daughters.* 1799–1800. Tempera on canvas. $10\frac{3}{4} \times 15\frac{1}{8}$ in. Washington, National Gallery of Art, Lessing J. Rosenwald Collection

111. *The Book of Job: So the Lord blessed the latter end of Job more than the beginning.* 1826.
Line engraving (proof). Platemark $8\frac{3}{8} \times 6\frac{5}{8}$ in. Cambridge, Fitzwilliam Museum

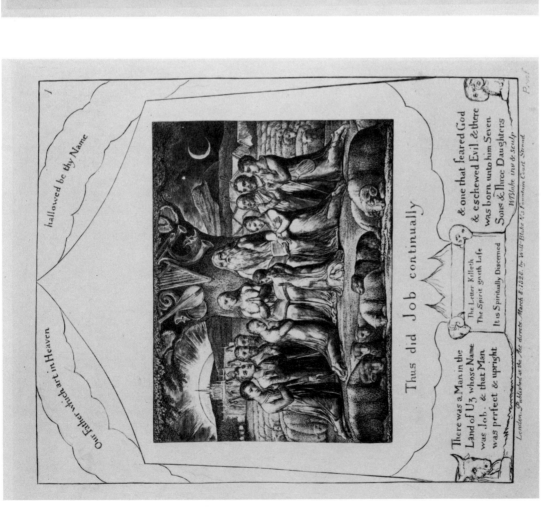

110. *The Book of Job: Thus did Job continually.* 1826. Line engraving (proof). Platemark
$8\frac{3}{8} \times 6\frac{5}{8}$ in. Cambridge, Fitzwilliam Museum

112. Dante's *Divine Comedy: Beatrice Addressing Dante from the Car*. 1824–7. Pen and watercolour. 14⅝ × 20¾ in. London, Tate Gallery

113. Dante's *Divine Comedy: The Rock Sculptured with the Recovery of the Ark and the Annunciation.* 1824–7. Pencil, pen and water-colour. 20¾ × 14¾ in. London, Tate Gallery

114. Dante's *Divine Comedy: Agnolo Brunelleschi and the Six-footed Serpent.* 1824–7. Pencil. 9¾ × 12⅞ in. San Marino, California, Henry E. Huntington Library and Art Gallery

HELL *Canto* 31

115. Dante's *Divine Comedy: The Complaint of the Giant Nimrod.* 1824–7. Pencil, pen and watercolour. 20¾ × 14¾ in. Cambridge, Massachusetts, Fogg Art Museum, Grenville L. Winthrop Bequest

116. Dante's *Divine Comedy: The Whirlwind of Lovers*. 1826–7. Line engraving. Platemark 10⅞ × 14 in. Engraved surface 9⅞ × 13¼ in. Washington, National Gallery of Art, Lessing J. Rosenwald Collection

Notes to the Plates

PLATE 1. *The Penance of Jane Shore in St Paul's Church.*

'This Drawing was done above Thirty years ago', according to the *Descriptive Catalogue*, which would place it before 1779, but the version to which Blake refers is almost certainly a smaller one, now in a private collection, and not this considerably more assured version, now in the Tate Gallery.

PLATE 2. *War (A Breach in a City).*

The earliest known version of *War* is now in the Carnegie Library, Pittsburgh.

PLATE 3. *Tiriel: Har and Heva Bathing.*

It has been suggested that the figure of Mnetha derives from Pellegrino Tibaldi; see Fitzwilliam Museum *William Blake* catalogue, p. 8.

PLATE 4. *Edward & Elenor.*

It may be that a connection exists between this engraving and an anonymous tragedy *Edward and Eleonora* advertised in a bookseller's catalogue in 1793 (*Blake Records*, p. 613). Perhaps a previously executed plate by Blake was found appropriate for the promotion of this book and accordingly redated.

PLATE 5. *Ezekiel.*

This engraving is a companion piece to the much improved second state of *Job*.

PLATE 9. *The Marriage of Heaven and Hell*, copy G, plate 11.

The treatment of the upper design shows how free Blake was to vary details in painting over his etched base. In some copies this scene is viewed from the mouth of a cave; in some the central object is a plant, in others a waterspout; sometimes a bearded face is seen within the plant or waterspout.

PLATE 10. *Visions of the Daughters of Albion*, plate ii, title-page.

The winged disc is a symbol of divinity in ancient Middle Eastern cylinder seals.

PLATE 12. *A Large Book of Designs*, 5: *Visions of the Daughters of Albion*, frontispiece.

This plate is an epitome of the whole *Visions of the Daughters of Albion*, but several lines are related to it more particularly:

> Bound back to back in Bromion's caves, terror & meekness dwell (2:5, Keynes, p. 190)

> 'Why does my Theotormon sit weeping upon the threshold' (2:21, Keynes, p. 190)

> 'Till she who burns with youth, and knows no fixed lot, is bound
> In spells of law to one she loathes?' (5:21–2, Keynes, p. 193)

PLATE 15. *Europe*, plate i, frontispiece.

When he prepared the heavens, I was there: when he set a compass upon the face of the depth. (Proverbs 8:27)

> He took the golden Compasses, prepar'd
> In God's Eternal store, to circumscribe
> This Universe, and all created things:
> One foot he centred, and the other turn'd
> Round through the vast profundity obscure,
> And said, thus far extend, thus far thy bounds,
> This be thy just circumference, O World.
> *Paradise Lost*, VII, 225–31

PLATE 20. *The Song of Los*, plate 5, and
PLATE 21. *Oberon and Titania.*

The prototype of both of these is an ink and wash drawing attributed to Robert Blake in Blake's *Notebook*. An adaptation of this design by Frederick J. Shields was used for the cover of the second edition of Gilchrist's *Life*.

PLATE 23. *A Small Book of Designs*, 3: *The Book of Urizen*, plate 17.

This design, originally plate 17 of *The Book of Urizen*, depicts the birth of Enitharmon from a globe of blood, originally the blood of Los. Blake also intended to bring this episode into *The Four Zoas*.

PLATE 26. *Hecate.*

The priestess enters, with her hair unbound,
And thrice invokes the powers below the ground.
Night, Erebus, and Chaos, she proclaims,
And threefold Hecate, with her hundred names,
And three Dianas . . .
The Works of Virgil, translated by John Dryden.
London, Oxford University Press, 1961, p. 231.

PLATE 29. *Nebuchadnezzar.*

Some very interesting sources and analogues of *Nebuchadnezzar* have been identified by Dr Bo Lindberg, among them a woodcut by Hans Weiditz dated 1531, in 'William Blakes Nebuchadnezzar och mänskoduret', *Taidehistoriallisia Tutkimuksia—Konsthistorika Studier 1.*

PLATE 31. *The Good and Evil Angels.*

In a watercolour version of this subject (Cecil Higgins Museum), the male figure is youthful and heroic; his eyes, as in *The Marriage*, are open. In another example of the colour-printed drawing (John Hay Whitney Collection), his eyes are open but his expression is woebegone. The two colour-printed drawings reverse the compositions of the versions in *The Marriage* and the watercolour.

PLATE 34. *Lucifer and the Pope in Hell.*

An uncoloured version of this print is in the British Museum. Compositionally, the design is closely related to the watercolour *The King of Babylon in Hell*, painted for Thomas Butts, and now in the Boston Museum of Fine Arts.

PLATE 35. Young's *Night Thoughts*, Night VIII, title-page.

The title of Night VIII is *Virtue's Apology*. But for Blake Virtue is synonymous with Rahab-Vala-Tirzah, and so he pictures her as the Whore of Babylon. The beast which she rides embodies the institutions of Church and State, as represented by its seven grotesque heads: judge, warrior, king, pope, emperor, bishop, priest. The picture as a whole is an epitome of the fallen world: 'Religion hid in War, a Dragon red & hidden Harlot' (*Jerusalem*, 89:53, Keynes, p. 735).

PLATE 36. Young's *Night Thoughts*: Night III, title-page.

The father, possibly Los or Albion, poisoned by the knowledge of Good and Evil, falls back against the Rock of the Decalogue. The mother, Enitharmon or Vala, tries to prevent the child from pursuing a joy. These elements are already present in the Lambeth books, but it would have taken an ideal reader-spectator to bring them together in 1797.

PLATE 42. *Vala or The Four Zoas*, p. 86.

This figure has been variously identified as Vala, Enitharmon, Rahab, and even Catherine Blake! What is most important is that she represents the triumphant Female Will, flaunting her sexual beauty.

PLATE 44. *Design for an Album:* Title-page for Blair's *Grave.*

Although sometimes referred to as a rejected title-page, it seems likely that this lovely drawing was not intended for engraving. We know that Cromek exhibited Blake's *Grave* drawings in London and that they were also exhibited in Birmingham. This title-page would have been appropriate for such a display.

PLATE 45. Blair's *Grave: Death's Door.*

Only a single impression of this relief etching, once owned by Samuel Palmer, is known to exist.

PLATE 47. *The spiritual form of Nelson guiding Leviathan.*

Despite all that is known about Blake's pacifist beliefs during his later period, some critics would still like to see this as a patriotic painting, thus putting themselves in the company of Robert Hunt and the *Examiner*. A glance at the black slave at Nelson's feet should be enough to confirm that this is a vision of 'War & its horrors & its Heroic Villains' (Keynes, p. 400).

What was once interpreted as a shock of hair in

Nelson's right hand (*Prophet*, p. 450; M. D. Paley, *Energy and the Imagination*, pp. 184–5) is actually a conventionalized firebrand or thunderbolt; cf. Michelangelo's drawing *The Fall of Phaethon*.

PLATE 48. *The spiritual form of Pitt, guiding Behemoth.*

In plate 91 of *Jerusalem* (Keynes, p. 738) the Spectre forms 'Leviathan/And Behemoth, the War by Sea enormous & the War/By Land astounding . . .' As Nelson is the appropriate hero for the first, so Pitt is for the second. Blunt (p. 38) points out that Pitt has a Buddhist halo. The irony here should be obvious.

PLATE 50. *The Last Judgment.*

Blake's *Last Judgment* painting is not known to exist. It is described by John Thomas Smith as 'containing upwards of one thousand figures, many of them wonderfully conceived and grandly drawn' (*Blake Records*, pp. 467–8). Blake seems to have worked on this large tempera for at least seventeen years. George Cumberland's son reported in 1815 that 'it is nearly as black as your hat—the only lights are those of a *Hellish Purple*' (*Blake Records*, p. 235); but Smith says, 'The lights of this extraordinary performance have the appearance of silver and gold; but upon Mrs Blake's assuring me that there was no silver used, I found, upon a closer examination, that a blue wash had been passed over those parts of the gilding which receded, and the lights of the forward objects, which were also of gold, were heightened with a warm colour, to give the appearance of the two metals.' Blake explained the symbolism of the painting in a fragmentary essay written in his *Notebook*, to which the editorial title 'A Vision of the Last Judgment' has been given (Keynes, pp. 604–17).

There are three highly finished *Last Judgment* drawings. The 1806 version is in the collection at Pollok House, Glasgow. A pen and wash drawing over pencil is in the Lessing J. Rosenwald Collection; it is reproduced with detailed discussion and a pictorial key by S. Foster Damon in *A Blake Dictionary*.

PLATE 52. *Milton*, copy B, plate 18 (*Census* 15).

Copy A: The disc behind grey Urizen-Jehovah is black. The figures on top are garbed respectively in grey, green, blue, pink and grey. There is green foliage in the background, as there is also in B and C. Copy B: The earth beneath Milton's left foot is green, and the mound beneath grey Urizen-Jehovah is also green, giving the Tables of the Law a more gravestone-like effect. The figures behind are pinkish white. Copy C: The earth, hummock and foreground are blue. Urizen-Jehovah wears blue. The tables are darker than in A and B—almost black. Figures are green, blue, flesh-colour, rose and blue. Copy D: Foreground and hummock are dark blue to black. Urizen-Jehovah is grey. Figures are blue, blue, rose, blue, yellow and gold—the sixth figure appears in D only. There is no green foliage, the background being maroon and gold.

PLATE 53. *Milton*, copy B, plate 1, title-page.

A and B display the graphic technique of stippling on the body, white line in the cloud, and horizontal lines in the background. The toes of Milton's left foot are firmly on the green earth, the heel in the air. His prominent eye makes him look rather scared. In B his hand goes into the cloud-vortex, but not in A. C is similar in most respects, but has some heightening in gold. In D the white lines, so prominent in the other copies, have been painted over. It has an overall effect more like that of a watercolour than of an etching. The stippling has been replaced by rounded contours. Milton's expression seems almost blasé. All the blues of A and B have disappeared, while the flames (absent from A and B) are pronounced. His hand goes into the vortex.

PLATE 54. *Milton*, copy D, plate 16 (*Census* 13).

The different treatment of this plate in the four copies is a good example of the different effects Blake achieved in each. In copy A Milton's body is very dark—even his garment is dark. His genitals are not visible. The disc of the Earth is all black, the sun yellow. The halo has a firm linear effect. White line is a marked feature here and in B, but in B Milton's body has the stippled texture it also has in the frontispiece, and it is almost rose-coloured. Both garment and belt are streaked with white lines. In B Milton's genitals are visible. His halo is a white nimbus. Again the Earth is black and the sun yellow. In both A and B the left foot does not touch the garment. C does not have the dark effect of A and B (though it is darker than D). Milton's genitals are visible. The few white streaks of his halo and garment are very much accentuated. Gold is inlaid in the solar disc. The Earth is not black but colour-printed in dark green and gold. In D Milton has rich ringlets of hair. His genitals are visible, his body flesh-coloured, his garment and belt white. His left foot treads on the garment. The Earth is black with white streaks on it. The halo is rosy.

PLATE 55. *Milton*, copy D, plate 37 (*Census* 33).

In A there is only the faint suggestion of a loincloth; in B the figure wears a transparent garment; in C and D he wears a green one. In A and B his body is very dark, almost like iron; it is flesh-coloured in D, and somewhat darker in C than in D.

PLATE 56. *Milton*, copy B, plate 42 (*Census* 38).

The two figures, flesh-coloured in copy D, are purplish and even black in A and in B (where much white-line effect is visible). In C the male is greenish, the female white to grey. His penis is distinctly visible only in A. The sky is blue in D, steel-coloured elsewhere, and the rock is parti-coloured in D alone, greenish elsewhere. The eagle is black with white line in all copies but D, where it is brown with some additional colouring.

PLATE 57. Milton's *Il Penseroso: Milton and the Spirit of Plato*.

It should be clear that some negative force is carried by almost every one of the images which Plato reveals to Milton. The three Fates (top) are the goddesses of this world for Blake; the couple bound back to back in the disc to our left are in the situation of Oothoon and Bromion; the weary-looking father-god in the

disc to our right seems hardly able to hold his compasses. Taken together, Venus, Jupiter and Mars (as identified in Blake's note, Keynes, p. 619) form another of Blake's unholy trinities. The water spirit at the lower right is entrapping an undine in his net, and the other elemental spirits also seem to be up to no good. As for Milton's 'thrice great *Hermes*', in *Jerusalem*, plate 91 we find the Spectre 'Repeating the Smaragdine Table of Hermes to draw Los down/Into the Indefinite . . .' (Keynes, p. 738)

PLATE 66. *A Spirit vaulting from a cloud*.

Related to, but not identical with, the picture with the same title exhibited by Blake in 1809.

PLATE 71. *The Characters in Spenser's 'Faerie Queene'*.

This painting was evidently intended as a companion to Blake's earlier *Canterbury Pilgrims*. It remained unsold during his lifetime, however, and was purchased by the Earl of Egremont from Mrs Blake. For an extensive analysis and discussion, see John E. Grant and Robert E. Brown, 'Blake's Vision of Spenser's *Faerie Queene*'. *Blake Newsletter*, VIII (1974–5), pp. 56–85.

PLATE 74. *The Pardon of Absalom*.

Blake had a special interest in Absalom as the disobedient son who in effect becomes his father by possessing his father's concubines. The engraving 'My Son, my Son!' in *The Gates of Paradise*, as well as the *Notebook* sketch for it and the related drawing in the British Museum, shows an Absalom figure who threatens his aged father with a spear. Fuzon in *The Book of Ahania* is another Absalom: he assumes the place of the father he thinks he has killed, only to be killed himself.

PLATE 85. *Theotormon Woven*.

The title of this drawing presents a puzzling problem, and were it not written in Blake's hand, we might be inclined to doubt it. Theotormon is *not* woven in any of Blake's known writings, while in Night I of *The Four Zoas* Tharmas sinks into the 'filmy Woof' of

Enion, and his Spectre is drawn forth 'from her shining loom/Of Vegetation' (Keynes, pp. 266, 267). The presence of the dome of St Paul's in the background leads Keynes to suggest a connection with the passage in Night VIII (Keynes, p. 342) where

>Enitharmon erected Looms in Luban's Gate
>And call'd the Looms Cathedron; in these Looms she wove the Spectres
>Bodies of Vegetation . . .
>>See *Pencil Drawings by William Blake* (London, Nonesuch, 1927) no. 23.

PLATE 86. *The Head of the Ghost of a Flea.*

This is one of the celebrated 'Visionary Heads' produced for the artist and astrologer John Varley between 1819 and 1825. Keynes (*Blake Studies*, p. 134) has shown that in this instance Blake's vision was influenced by an engraving in Robert Hooke's *Micrographia*.

PLATE 88. *Epitome of James Hervey's 'Meditations among the Tombs'.*

Blake had genuine admiration for James Hervey, who is one of the 'gentle Souls' who guard the southern gate of Jerusalem (Keynes, p. 712). Blake has written identifications of the various figures in the picture, chosen very selectively and in some instances inventively, from Hervey's *Meditations*. At our upper right WRATH is written, and at our upper left MERCY. The inscription above God the Father is 'God out of Christ is a Consuming Fire'. This doctrine comes from Jakob Boehme, who Blake says 'appear'd to me' with Paracelsus (Keynes, p. 799), as does the analysis of the Godhead into components of Love and Wrath.

PLATE 89. *'The Arlington Court Picture'.*

The original title of this picture is not known; nor are the circumstances by which it came into the possession of the Chichester family at Arlington Court, Devonshire, where it was discovered in 1947. For a detailed analysis, see Anne K. Mellor, *Blake's Human Form Divine*, Berkeley, University of California Press, 1974, pp. 256–70.

PLATE 91. *Genesis* MS., second title-page.

If completed, this rendition of Genesis would have been Blake's closest approach to a medieval illuminated manuscript. However, it was left as an incomplete fragment of eight pages, two of which are alternative title-pages. This second one is the more finished. Characteristically, Blake portrays the Evangelists as the Four Zoas. The Holy Ghost, to whom the Father points, is an athletic winged figure; and an aspiring haloed Adam—the Divine Humanity—occupies the dramatic centre.

PLATE 92. *The Man Sweeping the Interpreter's Parlour.*

'The *Interpreter* answered, This Parlour is the Heart of a Man that was never sanctified by the Sweet Grace of the Gospel: the Dust is his Original Sin, and Inward Corruptions that have defiled the whole Man. He that began to sweep it at first is the *Law*; but she that brought Water and did sprinkle it, is the *Gospel*.' As Keynes (*Separate Plates*, p. 32) points out, Blake has given the Law a Satanic aspect.

PLATE 96. *Jerusalem*, plate 1, frontispiece (proof).

This proof bears several passages which were expunged from the finished work. The reason Blake did so is not clear, for they are of considerable thematic importance. For the texts see Keynes, p. 620.

PLATE 98. *Jerusalem*, copy A, plate 31 (*Census* 35).

The upper figure of Christ (with stigmata clearly visible) derives from the flying figure of St Mark in Tintoretto's *Miracle of the Slave*. Here we have another example of Blake drawing on a source antipathetic to him, as if endeavouring to show how such a figure should really be executed.

PLATE 100. *Jerusalem*, copy A, plate 95.

The rising Albion trails a skirt-like garment of flesh that is about to be put off. (For details about the re-etching of part of this plate, see *Illuminated Blake*, p. 374.)

PLATE 115. Dante's *Divine Comedy: The Complaint of the Giant Nimrod.*

In his *Riposo*, Blake says, 'I have given, in the background, a building, which may be supposed the ruin of a Part of Nimrod's tower, which I conjecture to have spread over many Countries; for he ought to be reckon'd of the Giant brood.' (Keynes, p. 824). The tower is of course the Tower of Babel, assigned to Nimrod by the tradition which Dante also follows. 'What need hath the Lord of a hunter such as Moses says that Nimrod was, a mighty hunter before the Lord.' (Boehme, *Mysterium Magnum*, 35:22) Nimrod also figures in Swedenborg's *Arcana* I, and in *Paradise Lost*, XII, 24–62. According to Jacob Bryant's *New System*, 'It is said of Nimrod . . . that *the beginning of his kingdom was Babel*', and 'He is described as a gigantic, daring personage; a contemner of every thing divine.' (*A New System*, III [1776], pp. 33–6). The passage of the *Inferno* illustrated is xxxi, 40–78.

Glossary

Blake had, in common with some of his greatest contemporaries, a desire to convey his meaning through the creation of a myth. While Keats and Shelley, for example, attempted to invest the classical gods with new meaning, Blake made up his own names and terms. The result may at times appear obscure or confusing, but anyone who can appreciate the methods of Renaissance allegory is well equipped to appreciate the nature of Blake's enterprise. It is important to remember that Blake's symbols must be understood in context; they are not part of a puzzle in which each cipher has a fixed, immutable meaning. Bearing this in mind, the reader may find the following brief definitions helpful. For more detailed definitions the reader should refer to *A Blake Dictionary* by S. Foster Damon, 1965.

AHANIA is URIZEN's EMANATION and a fertility goddess whose attraction is so threatening to her consort that he casts her into the void.

ALBION is both England and humanity. Although capable of regeneration, he is usually seen in his fallen state, brooding on his own imagined sins, accusing sin in others, rejecting his emanation JERUSALEM, and punishing his brother LUVAH (as France).

BEULAH, Isaiah's name for the Promised Land (Heb. 'married'), is a name employed by John Bunyan as well as by Blake for the Earthly Paradise. In this harmonious, happy state, humanity finds rest; but this cannot be prolonged without deleterious results, as demonstrated by the senile Har and Heva of *Tiriel*. We are meant to go on to EDEN and the labours of Eternity.

CHURCHES are segments of the cycle of human history, going round in eternal circle from Adam to Luther.

CONTRARIES are powerful forces which in their striving against one another create progression. They are not to be confused with NEGATIONS, which merely repress or deny. Reason and Energy are contraries; the nation state is a negation.

The COVERING CHERUB is derived from Ezekiel 28. For Blake it is the monstrous Law that man has created and that now blocks his way back to Eden. It must be consumed at the Last Judgment.

The DAUGHTERS OF ALBION appear as victims in Blake's earlier works and as tormentors in the later ones. The two most important are the warlike Gwendolen and the false virgin-mother Cambel.

EDEN is not a passive state of bliss or a static paradise. It is a field of intellectual strife, of the interplay of human energies. The artist in the act of creation is already in Eden.

The EMANATION combines the loving, creative, and intuitive components of human identity. Without his emanation, the male becomes a ravening SPECTRE, as does Albion when he rejects Jerusalem.

ENION is an earth-mother whose children, LOS and ENITHARMON, reject her. Her male counterpart is THARMAS, the ZOA of the body.

ENITHARMON is the wife of Los, and so on one level is Catherine Blake. The myth of this quarrelling couple occupies much space in Blake's later works, but when they work together in harmony they produce beautiful 'embodied semblances'—the illuminated books. In Blake's myth Enitharmon represents Space and is associated with the moon.

The EYES OF GOD are successive manifestations of the Godhead in human history, seven in number from Lucifer, the SELFHOOD, to Jesus, the Sacrificer of Self. The eighth Eye, humanity itself, has not yet opened.

The FEMALE WILL is the negative aspect of Woman, as the Spectre is that of Man, striving for domination as tyrannical queen, cruel mistress, or demanding goddess.

GENERATION, a Platonic and Neo-Platonic term, is the STATE in which we live now, the world of repression and limit explored in *Songs of Experience*. From Generation we can go 'up' into Beulah or 'down' into ULRO, but we cannot get directly back into Eden.

GOLGONOOZA, the Spiritual Fourfold London, is a word compounded of Golgotha, the 'place of the skull' where Jesus was crucified, and 'ooze'—the primeval slime out of which life comes. Paradoxically, new life can come only from sacrifice of Self. Los continually labours to create Golgonooza from the materials of London, its form in the world of Generation.

JERUSALEM, a city yet a woman, is at the same time the emanation of Albion and the fulfilment of the human community. She is the Liberty to which man aspires.

LOS figures in Blake's illuminated books as the Eternal Prophet, as a worker in metals (a counterpart of the alchemical Vulcan) and as the creator of Time. He is sometimes closely associated with Blake himself. In his unfallen form, he is URTHONA (= 'earthowner'), but in the fallen world he is capable of error and sometimes does Urizen's work for him, as when he binds the adolescent ORC in *The Book of Urizen*. Yet, as he embodies the prophetic spirit, he alone can save Albion; in *Jerusalem* he becomes the active imaginative principle which fights to keep the Divine Vision.

LUVAH is the Zoa of passion, tormented by the nature-goddess VALA whom he adores. When, as the spirit of post-Revolutionary France, Luvah becomes warlike and tyrannical, he is replaced by Jesus, who descends wearing Luvah's robes of blood. At this point only an inner regeneration, what Gandhi called 'a change of heart', can save humanity.

The MUNDANE SHELL is the seemingly round but to Blake egg-shaped world *inside* which we live. In *Milton*, plate 33, it is diagrammed as intersecting the discs of all four fallen Zoas. When we are ripe, we hatch from it.

ORC (meaning 'killer whale') is the child of Los and Enitharmon. At first he represents revolutionary Energy as in *America*; later he is corrupted into the will-to-power as the French Revolution turns from Republic to tyranny, and he loses his human form and becomes a serpent. He literally burns out at the end of *The Four Zoas*.

SELFHOOD, a term derived from Jakob Boehme, denotes the will separated from organic connection with the rest of the self and with the community. When Blake's Milton recognizes his past errors, he declares 'I in my Selfhood am that Satan: I am that Evil One!' (Keynes, p. 496).

The SONS OF ALBION war against the primal father, first in self-defence but then to assert their own dominion. The most important of them are taken from Blake's own experience. Skofeld is named for Private John Scholfield, who accused Blake of seditious utterances at Felpham. Hyle (Gk. 'matter') is derived from the name of William Hayley, Blake's corporeal friend and spiritual enemy. Hand, the accuser, comes from the siglum of a pointing hand, used by the Hunt brothers in the *Examiner*, in which Blake's exhibition of 1809 was viciously attacked.

The SPECTRE is defined by its form rather than by its content. In content it may express such apparently opposed doctrines as rationalism or Calvinism, but in form the Spectre is a broken-off member which must continually attempt to dominate while at the same time feeling the effects of its incompleteness.

STATES are temporary conditions of being through which Individuals pass. Innocence and Experience are States, as is Satan.

THARMAS is the 'Parent pow'er' [*sic*] in *The Four Zoas* because he is the stream of physical sensation without which no human life can exist. His name is compounded of the River Thames and Doubting Thomas.

ULRO is the hell we create for ourselves when we assume that Generation is the only world that exists.

URIZEN's name is compounded of 'horizon' and 'your reason'. He is the force that quantifies and limits. As an ogrish father-god he writes the Law which no flesh can keep; then he weeps because he must punish his transgressing children. Yet he too has a place in the story: after the great synthesis at the end of *The Four Zoas*, he once more becomes the Prince of Light who goes forth to sow the seed of Eternal Science.

VALA ('veil'/ 'vale') is nature, not in the sense of the world of plants and animals a hypostasization. The *idea* of Nature as a governing principle is to Blake a self-tormenting delusion.

ZOAS (Gk. 'living creatures', from Revelation 4) are the four constituent faculties of man: Los, Luvah, Tharmas, and Urizen. Their corresponding emanations are Enitharmon, Vala, Enion, and Ahania. When the Zoas war against one another, the fallen world is created; when their hierarchy is re-established, man attains a higher innocence.

List of Plates

Europe, copy H, plate 11. 1794. Relief etching, uncoloured, grey wash. $9\frac{1}{2} \times 7$ in. Harvard University, Houghton Library (*Pl.* 17)
Ezekiel. 1794. Line engraving. $18\frac{1}{8} \times 21\frac{1}{4}$ in. London, British Museum (*Pl.* 5)

The Fall of Man. 1807. Watercolour. $19\frac{1}{4} \times 15\frac{1}{8}$ in. London, Victoria and Albert Museum (*Pl.* 49)
The Fertilization of Egypt. 1791. Line engraving after Fuseli for *The Botanic Garden* by Erasmus Darwin. $7\frac{3}{4} \times 5\frac{7}{8}$ in. Cambridge University Library (*Fig.* 2)
The First Book of Urizen, copy D, plate 11. 1794. Relief etching, colour-printed, with opaque pigments. $5\frac{3}{4} \times 4\frac{1}{8}$ in. London, British Museum (*Pl.* 22)
The First Book of Urizen, copy D, plate 21. 1794. Relief etching, some colour-printing, mostly coloured with watercolour. $6\frac{1}{2} \times 4$ in. London, British Museum (*Pl.* 24)
See also *A Small Book of Designs*, 3 (*Pl.* 23)
For Children: The Gates of Paradise, copy B. 1793. Line engravings. Original leaves $5\frac{1}{4} \times 4\frac{1}{8}$ in. Plate measurements vary from $3\frac{1}{4} \times 2\frac{5}{8}$ in. to $2 \times 1\frac{3}{4}$ in. London, British Museum (*Fig.* 5)
The Four and Twenty Elders Casting Their Crowns Before the Divine Throne. 1805. Pencil and watercolour. $14 \times 11\frac{1}{2}$ in. London, Tate Gallery (*Pl.* 82)

The Gates of Paradise, see *For Children*.
Genesis MS., second title-page. 1821 or later. Pencil with touches of watercolour. $14\frac{7}{8} \times 10\frac{3}{4}$ in. San Marino, California, Henry E. Huntington Library and Art Gallery (*Pl.* 91)
God Writing Upon the Tables of the Covenant. About 1805. Watercolour. $16\frac{1}{2} \times 13\frac{1}{2}$ in. Edinburgh, National Gallery of Scotland (*Pl.* 32)
The Good and Evil Angels. 1795. Colour-printed monotype, finished with pen and watercolour. $17\frac{1}{2} \times 23\frac{3}{8}$ in. London, Tate Gallery (*Pl.* 31)
The Grave, see Blair's *Grave*.
Gray's *Poems*: no. 11, *Ode on the Death of a Favourite Cat (Drowned in a Tub of Gold Fishes)*. 1798. Watercolour. $16\frac{3}{8} \times 12\frac{1}{2}$ in. Yale Center for British Art, Mr and Mrs Paul Mellon Collection (*Pl.* 40)
The Great Red Dragon and the Woman Clothed with the Sun. About 1805. Watercolour. $17\frac{1}{2} \times 13\frac{1}{2}$ in. The Brooklyn Museum (*Pl.* 85)

The Head of the Ghost of a Flea. 1819. Pencil. $7\frac{1}{2} \times 6$ in. London, Tate Gallery (*Pl.* 87)
Heads of the Poets: John Milton. About 1800–3. Tempera on canvas. $15\frac{3}{4} \times 35\frac{3}{4}$ in. Manchester City Art Gallery (*Pl.* 69)
Heads of the Poets: Edmund Spenser. 1800–3. Tempera on canvas. $16\frac{1}{2} \times 33$ in. Manchester City Art Gallery (*Pl.* 70)
Hecate. 1795. Colour-printed monotype, finished with pen and watercolour. $17\frac{1}{4} \times 22\frac{7}{8}$ in. London, Tate Gallery (*Pl.* 26)
'The Horse' from Hayley's *Ballads*. 1805. Line engraving. $4\frac{1}{4} \times 2\frac{3}{4}$ in. Harvard University, Houghton Library (*Fig.* 6)
The House of Death. 1795. Colour-printed monotype, finished with watercolour. $18\frac{7}{8} \times 23\frac{7}{8}$ in. London, Tate Gallery (*Pl.* 33)

Illustrations for Robert John Thornton's 'Pastorals' of Virgil: Imitation of Eclogue I, nos. 2–5. Wood engraving. Design area of each block measures approximately $1\frac{3}{8} \times 2\frac{7}{8}$ in. London, British Museum (*Fig.* 10)
Jerusalem, plate 1, frontispiece (proof). 1804–20. Relief etching printed in black and brown; lettering picked out in black, $8\frac{3}{4} \times 6\frac{3}{8}$ in. Sir Geoffrey Keynes Collection (*Pl.* 96)
Jerusalem, copy A, plate 2, title-page. 1804–20. Relief etching. $8\frac{3}{4} \times 6\frac{1}{4}$ in. London, British Museum (*Pl.* 97)
Study for *Jerusalem*, plate 25. Red crayon on ivory paper. $6\frac{1}{2} \times 9$ in. Cambridge, Massachusetts, Fogg Art Museum (*Pl.* 105)
Jerusalem, copy A, plate 25. 1804–20. Relief etching. $8\frac{3}{4} \times 6\frac{1}{4}$ in. London, British Museum (*Pl.* 104)
Jerusalem, plate 28 (trial proof). 1804–20. Relief etching. $8\frac{3}{4} \times 6\frac{1}{4}$ in. New York, Pierpont Morgan Library (*Pl.* 102)
Jerusalem, copy E, plate 28. 1804–20. Relief etching, coloured with watercolour and gold. $8\frac{3}{4} \times 6\frac{1}{4}$ in. Yale Center for British Art, Mr and Mrs Paul Mellon Collection (*Pl.* 103)
Jerusalem, copy A, plate 31 (*Census* 35). 1804–20. Relief etching. $8\frac{3}{4} \times 6\frac{1}{4}$ in. London, British Museum (*Pl.* 98)
Study for *Jerusalem*, plate 51. Pencil. $6\frac{1}{4} \times 13\frac{3}{8}$ in. Hamburg, Kunsthalle (*Pl.* 106)
Jerusalem, copy E, plate 51. 1804–20. Relief etching, coloured with watercolour and gold. $6\frac{1}{4} \times 8\frac{3}{4}$ in. Yale Center for British Art, Mr and Mrs Paul Mellon Collection (*Pl.* 107)
Jerusalem, copy F, plate 75. 1820–6. Relief etching. $8\frac{7}{8} \times 6\frac{1}{4}$ in. New York, Pierpont Morgan Library (*Pl.* 99)
Jerusalem, copy A, plate 95. 1804–20. Relief etching. $8\frac{7}{8} \times 5\frac{3}{8}$ in. London, British Museum (*Pl.* 100)
Jerusalem, copy E, plate 100. 1804–20. Relief etching, coloured with watercolour and gold. $8\frac{3}{4} \times 5\frac{3}{4}$ in. Yale Center for British Art, Mr and Mrs Paul Mellon Collection (*Pl.* 101)
Job and his Daughters. 1799–1800. Tempera on canvas. $10\frac{3}{4} \times 15\frac{1}{8}$ in. Washington, National Gallery of Art, Lessing J. Rosenwald Collection (*Pl.* 109)
Joseph of Arimathea among The Rocks of Albion. About 1809–20. Line engraving, second state. Platemark $10\frac{1}{8} \times 5\frac{1}{2}$ in. London, British Museum (*Pl.* 94)
The Judgment of Paris. 1811. Watercolour. $15\frac{1}{2} \times 18\frac{1}{2}$ in. London, British Museum (*Pl.* 90)
Laocoön. About 1818. Line engraving. Engraved surface $10\frac{3}{8} \times 8\frac{5}{8}$ in. Platemark $10\frac{3}{4} \times 9$ in. Sir Geoffrey Keynes Collection (*Pl.* 95)

A Large Book of Designs, 2: Our End is come. 1794–5. Line engraving, colour-printed. $8\frac{1}{2}\times4\frac{3}{4}$ in. London, British Museum (*Pl.* 27)

A Large Book of Designs, 5: Visions of the Daughters of Albion, frontispiece. About 1795. Colour-printed, finished with opaque pigments and watercolour. $6\frac{3}{4}\times4\frac{1}{4}$ in. London, British Museum (*Pl.* 12)

The Last Judgment. 1808. Watercolour and pen over pencil. $19\frac{7}{8}\times15\frac{3}{4}$ in. Petworth House, Sussex, The National Trust (*Pl.* 50)

The Last Supper. 1799–1800. Tempera on canvas. 9×12 in. Washington, National Gallery of Art, Lessing J. Rosenwald Collection (*Pl.* 80)

Lucifer and the Pope in Hell. About 1795 or earlier. Colour-printed line engraving. $7\frac{1}{4}\times9\frac{3}{4}$ in. San Marino, California, Henry E. Huntington Library and Art Gallery (*Pl.* 34)

Malevolence. 1799. Pen and watercolour. $11\frac{7}{8}\times8\frac{7}{8}$ in. Philadelphia Museum of Art. (*Pl.* 41)

The Man Sweeping the Interpreter's Parlour. 1821–2. Engraving on pewter, second state. $3\frac{1}{8}\times6\frac{1}{4}$ in. London, British Museum (*Pl.* 92)

The Marriage of Heaven and Hell, copy F, plate 1, title-page. 1790–3. Relief etching, colour-printed, finished and heightened with watercolour. $5\frac{3}{4}\times4$ in. New York, Pierpont Morgan Library (Thorne Collection) (*Pl.* 8)

The Marriage of Heaven and Hell, copy G, plate 11. 1790–3. Relief etching with watercolour, strengthened in ink. $5\frac{7}{8}\times4$ in. Harvard University, Houghton Library (*Pl.* 9)

Mary Magdalen at the Sepulchre. About 1805. Pen and indian ink with some watercolour. $16\frac{1}{4}\times12$ in. Yale Center for British Art, Mr and Mrs Paul Mellon Collection (*Pl.* 83)

Milton, copy B, plate 1, title-page. 1804–9. Relief etching, painted in watercolour. $6\frac{1}{4}\times4\frac{1}{4}$ in. San Marino, California, Henry E. Huntington Library and Art Gallery (*Pl.* 53)

Milton, copy D, plate 16 (*Census* 13). 1804–15. Relief etching, painted in watercolour and some gold. $6\frac{1}{4}\times4\frac{1}{4}$ in. Washington, Library of Congress, Lessing J. Rosenwald Collection (*Pl.* 54)

Milton, copy B, plate 18 (*Census* 15). 1804–9. Relief etching, painted in watercolour. $6\frac{3}{4}\times4\frac{1}{4}$ in. San Marino, California, Henry E. Huntington Library and Art Gallery (*Pl.* 52)

Milton, copy A, plate 32 (*Census* 29). 1804–9. Relief etching, painted in watercolour. $6\frac{1}{2}\times4\frac{1}{2}$ in. London, British Museum (*Fig.* 9)

Milton, copy D, plate 37 (*Census* 33). 1815. Relief etching, outlined in ink, painted in watercolour, opaque pigments and gold. $6\frac{5}{8}\times4\frac{3}{8}$ in. Washington, Library of Congress, Lessing J. Rosenwald Collection (*Pl.* 55)

Milton, copy B, plate 42 (*Census* 38). 1804–9. Relief etching, painted in watercolour. $6\frac{1}{4}\times4\frac{1}{2}$ in. San Marino, California, Henry E. Huntington Library and Art Gallery (*Pl.* 56)

Milton's *Comus: Comus with His Revellers.* About 1810–15. Pen and watercolour. $6\times4\frac{3}{4}$ in. Boston, Museum of Fine Arts (*Pl.* 64)

Milton's *Hymn on the Morning of Christ's Nativity: The Overthrow of Apollo and the Pagan Gods.* About 1815–16. Watercolour. $6\frac{1}{4}\times4\frac{7}{8}$ in. San Marino, California, Henry E. Huntington Library and Art Gallery (*Pl.* 63)

Milton's *Paradise Lost: The Creation of Eve.* 1808. Watercolour. $19\frac{3}{4}\times15\frac{3}{4}$ in. Boston, Museum of Fine Arts (*Pl.* 59)

Milton's *Paradise Lost: Satan Watching Adam and Eve.* 1808. Pen and watercolour. $20\times15\frac{1}{8}$ in. Boston, Museum of Fine Arts (*Pl.* 60)

Milton's *Paradise Regained: Christ Tempted by Satan to Turn the Stones Into Bread.* About 1816–18. Watercolour with indian ink and grey wash. $6\frac{5}{8}\times5\frac{1}{4}$ in. Cambridge, Fitzwilliam Museum (*Pl.* 62)

Milton's *Il Penseroso: Milton and the Spirit of Plato.* About 1816. Watercolour. $6\frac{3}{8}\times4\frac{7}{8}$ in. New York, Pierpont Morgan Library (*Pl.* 57)

Milton's *Il Penseroso: Milton in his Old Age.* About 1816. Watercolour. $6\frac{1}{4}\times4\frac{7}{8}$ in. New York, Pierpont Morgan Library (*Pl.* 58)

Mirth and her Companions. About 1816–20. Line and stipple engraving, second state. $6\frac{3}{4}\times5\frac{3}{8}$ in. Sir Geoffrey Keynes Collection (*Pl.* 61)

Moses Erecting the Brazen Serpent. About 1805. Pen and watercolour. $13\frac{3}{8}\times12\frac{3}{4}$ in. Boston, Museum of Fine Arts (*Pl.* 73)

Mrs Blake. After 1802. Pencil. $11\frac{1}{4}\times8\frac{3}{4}$ in. London, Tate Gallery (*Fig.* 8)

Nebuchadnezzar. 1795. Colour-printed monotype, finished with pen and watercolour. $16\frac{3}{4}\times23\frac{3}{4}$ in. Minneapolis Institute of Arts (*Pl.* 29)

Newton. 1795. Colour-printed monotype, finished with pen and watercolour. $17\frac{7}{8}\times22\frac{1}{4}$ in. London, Tate Gallery (*Pl.* 30)

Oberon and Titania. About 1793. Watercolour. $8\frac{3}{8}\times6\frac{1}{2}$ in. Private Collection (*Pl.* 21)

Our End is come, see *A Large Book of Designs,* 2 (*Pl.* 27)

The Pardon of Absalom. About 1800–5. Watercolour. $12\frac{1}{2}\times14\frac{3}{4}$ in. Bedford, Cecil Higgins Art Gallery (*Pl.* 74)

The Penance of Jane Shore in St Paul's Church. About 1793. Pen and watercolour. $9\frac{5}{8}\times11\frac{5}{8}$ in. London, Tate Gallery (*Pl.* 1)

Satan calling up his Legions. Not dated. Tempera on canvas. $21\frac{1}{4}\times16\frac{1}{2}$ in. London, Victoria and Albert Museum (*Pl.* 65)

Sir Jeffrey Chaucer and the nine and twenty Pilgrims on their journey to Canterbury. 1808. Tempera on canvas. $18\frac{1}{4}\times53\frac{3}{4}$ in. Glasgow, Pollok House (*Pl.* 67)

A Small Book of Designs, 3: The Book of Urizen, plate 17. 1795–6. Relief etching, colour-printed. $5\frac{3}{4}\times3\frac{5}{8}$ in. London, British Museum (*Pl.* 23)

The Song of Los, copy D, plate 1, frontispiece. 1795. Relief etching, colour-printed, with opaque pigments. $9\frac{1}{4} \times 6\frac{7}{8}$ in. London, British Museum (*Pl.* 18)

The Song of Los, copy A, plate 5. 1795. Relief etching, colour-printed, with opaque pigments. $9\frac{1}{8} \times 6\frac{3}{8}$ in. London, British Museum (*Pl.* 20)

Songs of Innocence and of Experience (1789–94), copy I, plate 39, *The Sick Rose*. 1793. Relief etching with watercolour. $4\frac{3}{8} \times 2\frac{5}{8}$ in. Harvard University, Houghton Library (Widener Collection) (*Pl.* 11)

Songs of Innocence and of Experience (1793–4), copy B, plates 9 and 10, *The Little Black Boy*. Relief etching, colour-printed, with watercolour. $4\frac{1}{4} \times 2\frac{5}{8}$ in. London, British Museum (*Pl.* 7)

A Spirit vaulting from a cloud. 1809. Pen, ink and watercolour. $9\frac{1}{8} \times 6\frac{3}{4}$ in. London, British Museum (*Pl.* 66)

The spiritual form of Nelson guiding Leviathan. About 1806–9. Tempera on canvas. $30 \times 24\frac{5}{8}$ in. London, Tate Gallery (*Pl.* 47)

The spiritual form of Pitt, guiding Behemoth. 1806–9. Tempera heightened with gold on canvas. $29\frac{1}{8} \times 24\frac{3}{4}$ in. London, Tate Gallery (*Pl.* 48)

Theotormon Woven. About 1806–20. Pencil. $4\frac{3}{8} \times 3$ in. London, Victoria and Albert Museum (*Pl.* 86)

There is No Natural Religion, b, copy L, plates 1, 2, 3, 4, 8, 9, 10, 12. About 1788. Relief etching, some plates touched with watercolour. Measurements vary from $2\frac{5}{8} \times 1\frac{3}{4}$ in. to $2 \times 1\frac{5}{8}$ in. Reproduced from the facsimile published by the William Blake Trust (*Fig.* 4)

Thornton's *Virgil*, see *Illustrations for Robert John Thornton's 'Pastorals' of Virgil* (*Fig.* 10)

Tiriel: Har and Heva Bathing. About 1785–9. Point of the brush, indian ink, grey wash. $7\frac{1}{4} \times 10\frac{3}{4}$ in. Cambridge, Fitzwilliam Museum (*Pl.* 3)

Vala or The Four Zoas, p. 86. 1797–1807. Pencil and crayon. Page size $16\frac{1}{8} \times 12\frac{5}{8}$ in. London, British Museum (*Pl.* 42)

The Virgin and Child in Egypt. 1810. Tempera on canvas. $28\frac{3}{4} \times 23\frac{3}{4}$ in. London, Victoria and Albert Museum (*Pl.* 78)

Visions of the Daughters of Albion, copy A, plate ii, title-page. 1793. Relief etching with watercolour. $6\frac{3}{8} \times 5\frac{1}{8}$ in. London, British Museum (*Pl.* 10). See also *A Large Book of Designs*, 5 (*Pl.* 12)

War (*A Breach in a City*, later version). 1805. Watercolour. $11\frac{3}{4} \times 15\frac{1}{8}$ in. Cambridge, Massachusetts, Fogg Art Museum, Grenville L. Winthrop Bequest (*Pl.* 2)

The Woman Taken in Adultery. About 1805. Watercolour over traces of pencil. $14 \times 14\frac{1}{8}$ in. Boston, Museum of Fine Arts (*Pl.* 81)

Young's *Night Thoughts*: Night III, title-page. 1795–6. Watercolour. $20\frac{1}{2} \times 15\frac{3}{4}$ in. London, British Museum (*Pl.* 36)

Young's *Night Thoughts*: Night VIII, title-page. 1795–6. Watercolour. $20\frac{1}{2} \times 15\frac{3}{4}$ in. London, British Museum (*Pl.* 35)

Young's *Night Thoughts*, p. 12. 1797. Intaglio engraving. $14\frac{7}{8} \times 12\frac{3}{8}$ in. London, British Museum (*Pl.* 37)

Young's *Night Thoughts*, p. 23. 1797. Intaglio engraving. $14\frac{1}{4} \times 11\frac{1}{8}$ in. Oxford, Ashmolean Museum (*Pl.* 38)

Young's *Night Thoughts*, p. 35. 1797. Intaglio engraving. $15\frac{1}{8} \times 12\frac{3}{8}$ in. Oxford, Ashmolean Museum (*Pl.* 39)

(b) Works by other artists

Catherine Blake: *Portrait of the Young William Blake*. About 1827–31. Pencil. $6\frac{1}{8} \times 4\frac{1}{8}$ in. Cambridge, Fitzwilliam Museum (*Fig.* 1)

J. S. Deville: *Life Mask of William Blake*. About 1807. Plaster. $11\frac{1}{2}$ in. high. Cambridge, Fitzwilliam Museum (*Fig.* 7)

John Linnell: *William Blake*. 1820. Pencil. $7\frac{3}{8} \times 6\frac{1}{8}$ in. Cambridge, Fitzwilliam Museum (*Fig.* 11)

Lewis Schiavonetti: Blair's *Grave: Death's Door*. Engraving after Blake. 1808. $9\frac{1}{2} \times 5\frac{1}{4}$ in. London, Victoria and Albert Museum (*Pl.* 46)

Index

Index of Blake's Works

Index of Names